GIRLS AUTO CLINIC

GLOVE BOX GUIDE

Patrice Banks

ILLUSTRATIONS BY DIANNE CASTILLO

Touchstone

New York London Toronto Sydney New Delhi

TOUCHSTONE

An Imprint of Simon & Schuster, Inc.
1230 Avenue of the Americas
New York, NY 10020

First Touchstone trade paperback edition September 2017

TOUCHSTONE and colophon are registered trademarks of Simon & Schuster, Inc.

For information about special discounts for bulk purchases, please contact Simon & Schuster Special Sales at 1-866-506-1949 or business@simonandschuster.com.

The Simon & Schuster Speakers Bureau can bring authors to your live event. For more information or to book an event, contact the Simon & Schuster Speakers Bureau at 866-248-3049 or visit our website at www.simonspeakers.com.

Interior design by Lorie Pagnozzi
Illustrations by Dianne Castillo

Manufactured in the United States of America

10 9 8 7 6 5 4 3 2 1

Library of Congress Cataloging-in-Publication Data is available.

ISBN 978-1-5011-4411-0
ISBN 978-1-5011-4412-7 (ebook)

To Edwin Regis of Guy's Auto Clinic—all in.

Contents

Part i
GET TO KNOW YOUR VEHICLE

Part ii
EVERYTHING YOU NEED TO KNOW
ABOUT HOW CARS WORK

Part iii
COMMON ROADSIDE PROBLEMS (AND A MINI BUYER'S GUIDE)

Pop Quiz: Test Your Auto Care IQ

Ready for a test of your auto care know-how? Don't worry—you're not going to be graded. The main purpose of this little quiz is to show that when it comes to car care, there are loads of myths, misconceptions, and downright dangerous ideas out there. Some are just plain false. But others were once best practice—rules that applied to older cars and are no longer true. As technology has changed, so have the facts. No wonder we wind up confused.

Can you identify some of the myths and half-truths that have stood the test of time? Let's see if you can figure out whether the following statements are myths, facts, or something in between—an old-school tip your dad, husband, boyfriend, or brother still tells you to do! This last category is my favorite. When women come to me with car care misconceptions they've picked up from the men in their lives, I set them straight. Then I have them call up the perpetrators and tell them how it really is.

1. A hair dryer/plunger can be used to remove a dent.

☐ MYTH

☐ FACT

2. You must change your engine oil every 3,000 miles.

☐ MYTH

☐ FACT

3. You should inflate your tires to the air pressure shown on the tires' sidewalls.

☐ MYTH

☐ FACT

4. If regular-grade fuel is good, premium must be better. Better for the engine and better for the drive.

☐ MYTH

☐ FACT

5. Topping off the gas will save you money and trips to the gas station.

☐ MYTH

☐ FACT

6. Driving your car in cold weather without first warming it up for several minutes will damage your engine.

☐ MYTH

☐ FACT

7. To keep your car warranty valid, you must perform regular maintenance at the dealership where you purchased your car.

☐ MYTH

☐ FACT

8. Keeping your car's windows down in the summer instead of using air-conditioning saves money on gas.

☐ MYTH

☐ FACT

9. You should buy an SUV, because bigger cars are safer than smaller cars.

☐ MYTH

☐ FACT

10. You should replace your tires in pairs when one of them fails.

☐ MYTH

☐ FACT

11. Talking on your cell phone while pumping gas can cause a fire or explosion.

☐ MYTH

☐ FACT

12. You'll get more gas for your money if you fill up in the morning.

☐ MYTH

☐ FACT

13. You must winterize your car for cold weather.

☐ MYTH

☐ FACT

14. Fuel and oil additives help with your car's performance.

☐ MYTH

☐ FACT

Answers

1. A hair dryer/plunger can be used to remove a dent.

FACT! Yes, a hair dryer or plunger can sometimes be used to remove minor or small dents in the body, hood, or bumper of your car. However, this trick will not work on all cars or in all instances. A dent's location, as well as the material on the affected area (aluminum, carbon fiber, plastic, fiberglass, or steel), might make at-home dent removal difficult. For instance, hair dryers or plungers won't work at all on aluminum cars.

2. You must change your engine oil every 3,000 miles.

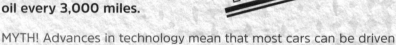

MYTH! Advances in technology mean that most cars can be driven at least 5,000 miles before an oil change is required.

3. You should inflate your tires to the air pressure shown on the tires' sidewalls.

MYTH! To be honest, I'm not sure how this misconception started. But at some point, tire manufacturers made the decision to print the *maximum allowable* pressure on the tire's sidewall, and ever since people have thought that this number represented *optimal* air pressure.

4. If regular-grade fuel is good, premium must be better. Better for the engine and better for the drive.

MYTH! Your engine is designed to burn fuel at a certain temperature. If it was designed to burn 87 octane or regular gas at a lower ignition temperature, there is no advantage to be gained by using 93—you will only be wasting money.

5. Topping off the gas will save you money and trips to the gas station.

MYTH! Do *not* top off the gas tank when you are filling up. You could be causing damage to your emissions system and wasting money.

6. Driving your car in cold weather without first warming it up for several minutes will damage your engine.

MYTH! One of the greatest myths in car care is the notion that you must warm up the car on cold winter mornings for five to ten minutes before you slide that puppy into drive. This myth made me hate winter that much more, and I even shelled out for a remote starter once. But warming up your car is no longer necessary. On modern cars (anything made in the past twenty years), you're not doing the engine any harm by taking off from a cold start. All you're really doing by "warming up your car" is wasting gas and making yourself late for work. So spend that extra ten minutes getting some coffee or getting more sleep.

   Please be warned, this isn't an excuse to hit D, then take off like you're racing Jeff Gordon. Slowly take off and drive gently. Essentially, you *are* warming up the car during your first few minutes of driving.

Disclaimer: If it's crazy cold out, like 20 degrees Fahrenheit or lower, warming up your car for two minutes helps the oil circulate through the engine.

7. To keep your car warranty valid, you must perform regular maintenance at the dealership where you purchased your car.

MYTH! This is a huge misconception, one that can make you feel locked in to going to a dealership for maintenance and repairs. As long as maintenance is performed on the schedule specified in your owner's manual, you can take your car to any shop. Don't forget to document all work in case you run into any warranty issues. And make sure you understand your car's warranty before you buy it.

8. Keeping your car's windows down in the summer instead of using air-conditioning saves money on gas.

MYTH (somewhat). I suffered so much as a child, my legs sticking to a searing leather seat in the heat of an East Coast summer. I thought I was going to faint in the hot car my mom's boyfriend drove us around in somewhere between July and Hell. If only I knew then what I know now. . . . Yes, it is correct that the AC uses gas. But driving with the windows down at speeds greater than 35 miles per hour causes the car to use more gas than if the windows were up. At faster speeds, the car is cutting through wind resistance as it drives, causing it to drag or slow down if windows are down. The engine has to work hard to cut through wind resistance at these speeds, and that requires more gas.

   Cars are aerodynamically designed to reduce drag, but only if we keep the windows closed. Plus, the amount of gas used by the AC system is not significant. Be comfortable, and don't let your passengers suffer like I did.

9. You should buy an SUV, because bigger cars are safer than smaller cars.

MYTH (somewhat). History has shown that bigger cars fare better in head-on collisions than smaller cars. But this doesn't mean that lighter vehicles are unsafe, and today's small cars are safer than ever. Choose a car that has performed well in the various government and insurance industry crash tests.

10. You should replace your tires in pairs when one of them fails.

FACT! Many shops and mechanics recommend replacing tires in pairs to ensure that all tires have the same tread depth. I know, I know—tires are expensive. So you could get away with replacing just one, especially on front- and rear-wheel-drive transmission models and/or if your other tire has a lot of remaining tread depth or is fairly new. But it is best practice to match your replacement tires to the brand, size, and speed rating of the original tires on the car.

All-wheel-drive vehicles require all four tires to be replaced, and I recommend replacing tires on four-wheel-drive vehicles in pairs.

11. Talking on your cell phone while pumping gas can cause a fire or explosion.

MYTH! The rare exploding cell phone with a malfunctioning battery may trigger massive recalls, but there is no evidence that a normally functioning cell phone can ignite fuel vapors. Don't smoke at the pump, though!

12. You'll get more gas for your money if you fill up in the morning.

MYTH! A few years ago I saw this gas myth floating around on Facebook in several memes. Yes, gas does turn into a vapor when it's hot (i.e., during the day), but once it's in your fuel tank, vapor collection systems send any vapors through a carbon-filled canister and then back into the engine. Also, gas is pretty much the same temperature no matter what the time of day, because a gas station's tanks are underground. A related myth? You shouldn't pump gas while a tanker is delivering at the station. Deliveries from tanker trucks do stir up particles of dirt and sludge in gasoline storage tanks, but this isn't much of an issue for our cars. Gas stations are required to install filters to trap dirt and sludge, and modern automobiles are also equipped with fuel filters, so a bit of stirred-up dirt doesn't have much potential to adversely affect your car. What *can* do damage to your fuel pump is leaving your gas tank below a quarter of a tank often. Moral of the story: Buy gas when you need it—there is no right time of day.

13. You must winterize your car for cold weather.

MYTH! Unless you live somewhere that gets monster snowstorms, there isn't much, if any, winterization that falls outside a normal maintenance schedule. Maintenance on brakes, tires, windshield wipers, and fluids should be performed on schedule, no matter the season. M+S (mud and snow) tires are all-season tires and work fine in most areas with light snow and ice. Snow tires and chains are for people who live in Wisconsin. But batteries hate to start in the cold, so if your battery is getting to the end of its life (four to six years), yes, you may want to be proactive and replace it before winter hits.

14. Fuel and oil additives help with your car's performance.

MYTH/FACT! *Fuel* additives are really only useful for high-performing sports cars—skip them if you don't have one. *Engine oil* additives and synthetic oil (see page 97 to find out more about the differences) won't prolong the life of the engine, but may provide added protection if you tend to wait long amounts of time between oil changes, or as the car ages. *Transmission oil* additives can be useful if you are having issues with a transmission slipping.

How did you do? If you bombed, there is absolutely no shame in your game. With all these car care myths, rumors, and half-true memes making the rounds, it's no wonder so many drivers are confused about the best way to care for their rides. But even if you aced this little quiz, I hope you learned a few things as well. The mission of Girls Auto Clinic is to educate female drivers, whatever their starting auto IQ.

Now buckle up and let's ride.

Introduction

My name is Patrice Banks, and I'm a former auto airhead. Not too long ago, when it came to my relationships with cars, I was a hot mess.

I'd always been a confident driver, the kind of aggressive lane changer and high-functioning parallel parker who'd burn rubber and curse out your grandmother to shave a couple of minutes off a ride through city traffic. But as far as auto maintenance and repairs, I was clueless. I was the walking stereotype of a female automotive consumer, a grown woman who needed a man to help her anytime anything went wrong with her car. Not just the mechanic at the shop, but also the boyfriend or father figure or friend who'd have to tell me it was *way* past time to get my tires changed or my engine looked at, and keep on badgering me about it until I finally dragged myself to the shop. I once drove around for four months in a heap that was straight-up leaking oil and smoking. Sure, I was putting myself through college and couldn't afford an expensive repair. But generally, I was the kind of driver whose stomach would drop anytime a dashboard light came on or a loud rattle escaped from under the hood. Instead of dealing with it, I'd say a silent prayer willing the problem to magically fix itself.

What's amazing about my auto airhead past is that I spent my pre–Auto Clinic career as a materials engineering consultant for one of the world's largest chemical companies. Part of my job was performing root-cause failure analysis on million-dollar pieces of manufacturing equipment. But was I interested in the root causes of failure in the cars I drove into the ground? Not so much.

"Car needs an oil change, but I'm going to get a mani-pedi instead."

That's a Facebook status I posted one day back when I was still work-ing at my job full-time. Knowing my silly little post would provoke some spirited dialogue, I headed off to my mani-pedi with a bounce in my step. Sure enough, I got back to my desk to find comments like "This is why women shouldn't drive," "Patrice, you're going to get stuck on the side of the road with a blown engine!" or "Whatever, at least she'll look cute when she's thumbing it for a ride." Of course the ladies had my back.

At the time I thought this was *hilarious*. I still do. But that anec-dote has also become part of the story I tell about my transformation from auto airhead to bona fide ♩#shecanic [she-kan-ik].

Back then, a regular day on the job for me was climbing up tow-ers a hundred feet in the air in coveralls, a hard hat, and steel-toed boots to check on huge tanks filled with hydrochloric acid. Yet I was so intimidated by my car that I prioritized getting my nails done over protecting a $25,000 investment.

Sounds bad, right? But if you bought this book, I'm guessing it might also sound familiar.

Women generally don't have the happiest, healthiest relationships with their cars, or with their mechanics. This might not cause real stress until that check-engine light comes on or a cloud of white smoke starts blowing up from under the hood. But our discomfort around the topic of our cars manifests itself in all kinds of little ways on a regular basis. For many of us, it takes the form of a pattern of avoidance that can result in costly repairs down the line.

You don't have to dig too deep to find out why so many women feel powerless when their cars break down. Despite the fact that women are the automotive industry's number one customers, there are vir tually no women working in the front lines of the industry. It's no wonder 77 percent of drivers believe women are more likely to be misunderstood and/or taken advantage of when bringing their cars in for service. We're walking into a man's world, grudgingly handing over our credit cards for repairs we don't understand as we tip-toe around with a serious lack of education about the 4,000-pound hunks of steel we have parked in our driveways.

That's a big part of why I went back to school to become a certified auto mechanic. My mission is to change the status quo, through the information in this book, the workshops I lead, and the inclusive atmosphere women encounter when they come to visit my shop and have their cars tended to by knowledgeable female mechanics.

My goal is to bring women along the path I traveled, wherever they are on the spectrum from auto airhead to car-care pro.

Building a Workshop

I skipped class at auto tech school to hold the very first Girls Auto Clinic workshop—a beta clinic that took place in a parking lot at the University of Delaware, where about twenty sorority members gathered on a crazy hot day in April 2013.

I've held more than forty workshops since then, and they always fill up fast.

We gather in parking lots, and women bring their cars so that we can take a hands-on look at the issues they have questions about. We start by congregating around a table stacked with a bunch of parts—brake lines, brake pads, rotors, belts, tie-rod ends, spark plugs, air filters—all in various conditions. And just as mechanics diagnose a lot of what's going on with a car by looking, listening, and touching, we do the same. We feel and examine the parts, comparing a worn brake pad that needs to be replaced and one that's brand-new or midway through its life cycle.

After show-and-tell, the first thing we do is learn to pop our hoods. So many women are embarrassed about the fact that they don't know how to do this, but I always emphasize that a Girls Auto Clinic workshop is a safe space. There are no questions too dumb, no maintenance flubs too gory.

Then we take a look under the hood and see what's going on in there. We learn which car parts can be touched and which should be handled only by a mechanic. I also demonstrate how to safely and confidently execute maintenance tasks and emergency fixes, such as jump-starting a car, adding coolant to your system, changing your air filter, and measuring tire wear and air pressure. (You'll find those skills in the color-coded DIY sections in the relevant chapters.)

Often women come in asking about a specific repair—they've gotten a quote from a mechanic and want to know whether I think they're being overcharged, or they want to know whether the repair their mechanic recommended is actually essential. One of the most common questions is, should they be changing their own oil? (The answer is: probably not. Sure, you could buy five quarts of oil and an oil filter from your local parts store for the same thirty dollars a mechanic would charge for the repair. But you would still need tools and the proper equipment to jack up the vehicle.)

The book you're holding in your hands grew out of a pamphlet I started handing out at those workshops. Just like my workshops, it's meant to empower women to take ownership over the care of their cars, and to replace the fear and anxiety that surrounds the subject with some know-how and a can-do approach.

A Brief Personal History of Car Ownership

I didn't grow up around cars. My family couldn't afford one. I was raised by a single mother who walked four miles to work, each way, in the blue-collar town of Phoenixville, Pennsylvania.

The first car in my household was mine, and I worked my way through a long list of high school jobs to save up for it. Getting that first car was a *very* big deal. Since no one in my immediate family drove, my grandpa, my pop-pop, taught me how in his dark green boat of a Buick.

After I'd gotten my license, he took me to the Honda dealership in Pottstown. Everyone had been telling us that Hondas lasted forever, but we ended up with a used 1988 Chevy Cavalier that was brown all the way through, inside and out. Not the most desirable color for a teenage girl, but I loved my "poop car." It's still my favorite to this day. We worked out a plan so that my pop-pop paid the $2,500 up front and I paid him back in monthly installments. I gave him the last check just before I headed off to college at Lehigh, in the town of Bethlehem, Pennsylvania. But you couldn't take your car with you the first year of school, so it sat parked on the street outside at my mom's house, until one day I let my boyfriend use it.

Big mistake. Let this be the first lesson of the *Girls Auto Clinic Glove Box Guide*: Unless he's a certified mechanic, never assume a man knows more about your car than you do. And don't let a man drive your car unless you happen to share a bank account or have access to his PIN.

On that particular day, the car started overheating and the engine shut off. Not his fault. But what happened next was avoidable. Instead of calling for help or popping the hood to see what was going on, he waited until the engine cooled down and then turned the car back on. It overheated and shut off again, a cycle that recurred a few more times on the way home. Each time he waited it out and restarted the car.

Turned out a loose hose had caused a large coolant leak. That was maybe a thirty-dollar repair at the time. But because the boyfriend continued to drive, he burned out the engine.

And that was it for my favorite car.

The auto airhead boyfriend didn't last too much longer after that. But not just because of the car.

My first car out of college was a brand-new, hunter green Ford Explorer that I financed myself. Hunter was her name. At the time I was living and working in West Virginia, which meant I made frequent trips home to Philly and racked up 65,000 miles in no time. Of course, I did absolutely zero maintenance beyond the oil changes I'd put off for months.

After I'd had the car for a couple of years, the O/D light on my dashboard started blinking. I had no idea what that meant, so I rushed to get help from a friend I'd met at the gym who happened to sell cars at the local Ford dealership. The service guys there told me the O/D light had to do with my transmission, and (drumroll) it was going to cost $1,700 to fix, something about a solenoid valve failing. "These things just go," I was told.

My heart skipped a beat, and not in a good way. I told them that was crazy, particularly since I had a warranty on the car, so as far as I could see the cost of the repair should be somewhere in the range of zero dollars, give or take.

Turned out my warranty expired after 60,000 miles, which I'd already exceeded.

I flew into a rage, then promptly melted down into tears. I was two years out of college, swimming in loans, and definitely not prepared for four-figure surprises.

My friend took pity on me and talked the dealership guys down to $1,200, and I sucked it up and handed over my credit card with a sinking feeling in my gut.

But when I got the car back, wouldn't you know it—there was a whole new problem. Now the car would shake anytime I was in park or neutral. Damn! These guys had messed up my ride instead of fixing it.

Back to the dealership I went, and one week later I got more frustrating news.

"We didn't do anything to cause the shaking. It probably has something to do with the way you take care of the car." Maybe it was related to my using regular gas instead of premium, they suggested.

Now I was *pissed*. These guys were clearly just trying to pin the problem on me. But maybe they were right? Had my auto airhead ways caused all of Hunter's problems? I felt defeated.

But I kept on driving the car over the next ten months.

Guess what happened after those ten months passed?

The O/D light came back on.

Yeah.

I took the car back to the dealership in a rage. And here is what they told me: "We only warranty our parts for ten thousand miles." I'd gone twelve, so the charge was going to be . . . let's see here, another $1,200.

There were other issues I'd been ignoring, too, and their origins were less mysterious. I'd driven that thing so hard and done so little maintenance on it that a whole bunch of repairs had accumulated. I'd run the tires ragged, driving more than 65,000 miles without getting a single one changed. Tires last only about 50,000 to 60,000 miles, so it's pretty amazing that I didn't catch a flat or skid out on one of those 500-mile drives across state lines. A mechanic had looked the car over and told me that I needed new tires, bad—my tires were bald, the car was unsafe to drive—not to mention new brakes and rotors, for a cost somewhere north of a grand. You'd think a safety warning would have spurred me into action, but nope. I made a mental note to take care of the issue as soon as it was convenient for me to do so, and then of course procrastinated instead. One day my best friend's dad caught sight of my car just as I was about to head out from DC to Philly. "Oh my god, Patrice," he cried, "those tires aren't going to get you back to Philly!"

Part of the reason I neglected all these repairs was the high repair bills. But I also hated the automotive repair experience. . . . I was filled with shame for neglecting my car and had no idea which repairs were really necessary. Was I being talked into something because I was an easy mark, a woman who obviously didn't know anything about cars? Was the cost fair? I had no idea. To top it off, I'd have to sit in some boring, uncomfortable waiting room watching *Maury* or CNN while the problems were being diagnosed? I'll pass, thanks.

One thing I did know was this stuff with the O/D light was total and utter BS.

I was so mad I traded that car in.

I tried another tactic to cure my car ownership blues, leasing a car for the first time, another Ford from that very same dealership.

Don't judge. They told me they would hook me up in return for all my troubles, and my friend said I seemed like a good candidate for a lease. I would have to cover only minor maintenance costs and wouldn't have to worry about repairs, and we could even roll over my unfinished payments on the first car. Knowing my auto airhead ways, he thought this might be the best option for me. And he assured me that I could just turn the car in when my lease was up.

Which is exactly what I did. Three years later, a barely maintained Ford in need of new rotors, brakes, tires, and more rolled up to that dealership, and its lessee walked in, dropped the keys off with a salesman, and ghosted past without even stopping by the cashier.

My next car was a Kia Sorento, and despite giving it the usual Patrice treatment, I never had any real problems with it. After the experience I'd had with the Ford, part of the reason I chose the Kia was the fantastic ten-year, 100,000-mile warranty. Of course, the car with the best warranty winds up being the one I never had problems with.

The Story of How I Became an Auto Mechanic

I couldn't find a female mechanic near me, so I decided to become one. That's the short version of the story, but the longer version begins six years ago, with an entrepreneurial itch.

I'd just moved from the Delaware suburbs to Philly, where I began meeting all these smart, independent women who were out there doing their thing—riding and racing motorcycles, building their own businesses, starting catering companies, creating real estate empires, and more. Being exposed to this wider social network gave me a jolt, made me realize that I wanted to create something, too. After ten years at DuPont I was ready for the next step in my career, or maybe a 180-degree flip. I wasn't quite sure which direction to turn, but I knew from the start that I wanted to do something empowering for women.

I'd gotten a lot of satisfaction out of leading DuPont's Explore Engineering program, an initiative designed to get high school girls interested in fields related to STEM (science, technology, engineering, and math). At my high school in Phoenixville, I'd been the only minority on the AP track. Most of the other students of color wound up in trade schools, and there was little to no financial or practical support in my less-than-stable household. My mother was on and off welfare, with a string of sometimes abusive boyfriends drifting through the house. Let's just say that without the support of my grandfather and a few high school teachers and counselors who took an interest in me, my life would have turned out *very* differently. By my early thirties, I was a college-educated homeowner (both firsts in my immediate family) with a career. It was time to give back.

I started toying with the notion of founding an informal women's university, a book club alternative where a group of women would meet once a month to learn the skills we'd typically pay men to take care of—anything from fixing leaking toilets to using automatic tools, from unclogging a drain to investing money or playing poker. Because I'd been meeting some women who were finding success online, the book club idea morphed into a blog.

I'd heard Tyra Banks tell this story about how, when she was developing her first talk show, she wanted to build up a log of a hundred ideas to make sure her concept had longevity. I decided that I'd do the same. I began cataloging topics for my blog. And I started asking women what they wished they knew more about. Anytime I'd meet a woman—over cocktails at a networking function, paying a cashier for my daily latte, or making small talk at the gym—I'd ask her: "What do you wish you knew about that you usually have to pay a man to take care of?"

Overwhelmingly, women's responses revolved around cars.

Without prompting, they'd say they wanted to learn more about their cars and feel better about the car-related decisions they made. They didn't feel good when they left the shop. They never knew if they'd made the right decision and didn't like the fact that they didn't know what to do in the event of an emergency. One high-ranking engineering colleague told me that when the mechanic called, she'd say, "Let me give you my husband's number so you can speak to him directly." Not exactly a recipe for empowerment.

The more I thought about it, the more sense it made. Cars were such a pain point in so many of our lives. And the stakes were pretty high, given the expense of purchasing and maintaining a vehicle. My own history was telling. If a science- and math-loving engineer who'd been trained to understand complex manufacturing equipment was so uncomfortable around the subject of her car that she'd rather avoid a much-needed oil change than face her mechanic, other women had to be feeling the same way. More and more it started to feel fated, like my ridiculous car history was some kind of a sign about what I was meant to do.

Looking around to see what resources already existed, I asked the hive whether anyone knew of a female mechanic in the area. Would the stats I'd been reading about the auto industry check out? Sure enough, not a single one of my fifteen hundred friends was able to recommend someone. I looked online and found a grand total of five searchable female mechanics in the United States, but none, as far as I could see, who worked in Philly.

That settled things. At the age of thirty-two, I enrolled as a student in automotive technology at Delaware Technical Community College.

On top of being the only woman, I was the oldest kid in the class, putting in a full day at my desk job at DuPont and then driving over to the school for night classes. There were a couple of people starting second careers, but mostly it was eighteen- and nineteen-year-old guys just out of high school. I didn't care. If anything, being the lone woman in the environment just underscored my motivation for being there.

The fact that I loved the material didn't hurt. Surprise, surprise. Once I turned my attention to it, my engineer brain took to the subject like a fish to water.

Despite my complete and total disregard for every car I'd ever owned, now that I had access to real information about cars, I was that kid in the front row with her hand raised. The auto airhead had become an auto fiend. A lot of my classmates had been working around cars their whole lives, and some of the material was so rote to them that they didn't really question it. But I always wanted to break down the why, trying to grasp the mechanics at the simplest, most elemental level.

I was still living my double life, getting dressed up for my job in corporate America, then changing into sweats and work boots to work on cars in the school's garage, the "lab" where we'd put our classroom knowledge into practice. One day I showed up to school without my change of clothes. I wasn't going to let a footwear issue come between me and a night's work, so I just threw on a sweatshirt over my blouse and got down under the car in my heels to pull out the starter. A fellow student snapped a pic of my heels sticking out from under the car, and a logo was born. A designer and I eventually turned the shoes red, for a bright pop of color. And the rest is history, laced with a little bit of regret from my toes.

For the record: I do not perform nor do I recommend performing extensive car repairs in high heels! But a girl boss does what she needs to do to get the job done. In heels, flats, or boots. This budding entrepreneur is looking out for her brand, and the red heels have become my signature.

While still in auto tech school, I started looking around for a shop that would let me work for free, to give me the experience I'd need in order to run a shop of my own. I cold-called dealerships and shops and asked advisers, friends, and co-workers for suggestions of places where I could barter my skills as a business-minded engineer for the chance to gain some real-world experience. I got turned down three times before finding someone who was open to the idea.

Some shop owners were afraid I'd steal customers. One owner's wife was threatened by the notion of another woman being around her man all day. But finally Edwin Regis, the owner of a place called Guy's Auto Clinic, gave me a yes.

I know. It seems too obvious. Only Guy was the name of Edwin's dad, the original owner of the shop.

I started working there nights and weekends, helping Edwin with the business side of things and cutting my teeth on small repairs, oil changes, and tire rotations. We ended up working so well together that we decided to partner. Edwin had been around cars since he was twelve, and he had the breadth of experience I needed in order to start up a business in an area where I was a complete novice.

Five years after I entered auto tech school, the very first Girls Auto Clinic shop opened its doors in the fair city of Philadelphia. We're fully operational, handling brake and rotor replacements, power steering jobs, alignments—the whole nine yards. With three full-time female mechanics and some helpers, we had nearly a hundred customers in our first month alone. Our female customers are so excited to watch us work and be a part of this movement that some come back with their daughters. And we've helped a handful of male customers, too.

It's a dream come true.

You don't have to go to school and become an auto technician, like I did, to grow into the confident and competent ♪#shecanics you ultimately want to be. The goal of this book isn't to have you covered in oil smudges as you dismantle your engine in your driveway, though you may get your hands dirty and break a nail or two (especially if you follow along with the handy, color-coded DIY pages sprinkled throughout this book). The truth is that it takes only a basic level of car knowledge to get to where you want to be. You don't have to read pages and pages of text that sounds like it was written by and for engineers and mechanics to become an informed and responsible car owner. And you don't need a technical degree in order to understand how cars work—though if you're interested in getting into the auto tech industry and becoming one of the heavy lifters, please get in touch.

An empowered ♪#shecanic loves company, so check out our Facebook community to join the movement, post questions, learn about workshops in your area, and share resources with other members online. Don't forget to follow us on Instagram, Twitter, and Facebook @girlsautoclinic for the latest and greatest updates from your favorite mechanic in heels and her team of history-making female mechanics.

Becoming a 𝄋#shecanic

Not long after I started Girls Auto Clinic, I realized that the company I was building had the potential to become a movement—and that I needed a name for the car-savvy ladies who were sounding off on our message boards and preaching the GAC mission to their families and friends. What is a 𝄋#shecanic, and what exactly is her skill set? Glad you asked! Whether you're a first-time car owner, a lifelong leaser, a black-belt parallel parker, or a serial auto shop dodger, you've come to the right place.

A 𝄋#shecanic is a woman of any age who has mastered the mechanics of "Yes, I can" and uses those building blocks to get to "Yes, I did."

She knows she is smart enough to understand and care for her car to the extent required of a well-educated consumer.

She treats her car as she does her own body. She doesn't try to be her own physician, but she wants to know how to maintain her health and prevent sickness and disease.

She has empowered herself to take charge of the fate of her vehicle, and she inspires other women to do the same.

And finally . . .

A 𝄋#shecanic no longer fears the auto repair shop or the auto mechanic!

Part i

GET TO KNOW YOUR VEHICLE

Changing Your Vehicular Relationship Status

What are the characteristics of a good relationship? Commitment, consistency, communication . . . These are the qualities we expect from our significant others, partners, and friends. Stop and think about the relationship you have with your car. How well do you know your vehicle? Do you listen to her when she talks to you? Are you committed to taking care of her when she is in need? Are you loyal to your car, taking her to the same, trusted mechanic for repairs? Or do you treat your car like your least-favorite ex treated you?

We've all felt the frustration of a difficult relationship that doesn't fulfill our needs. But it's rarely a one-way street. You get what you give, and the same goes for your car: Do right by your ride and it will do right by you.

It's time to turn your car from a frenemy into your new best friend. And turning your relationship around starts with my five-step program.

Step 1: Renew your commitment. Your car is your baby, and you hereby pledge to care for it, in sickness and in health. You commit to providing for your car as needed, to the best of your ability.

Step 2: Know your car. One of the things we want the most in our close relationships is to be known. To have our feelings, likes and dislikes, and quirks and idiosyncrasies understood and accepted. Know your vehicle and your maintenance schedule (see page 22), and you'll be prepared for any craziness that comes your way.

Step 3: Stop seeing other people. There's a very important third party involved in this romance—your mechanic. A good relationship demands loyalty, and loyalty to your car means loyalty to a quality mechanic and a high standard of care. Stop shop-hopping! There's little to be gained from hopping around from mechanic to mechanic in search of deals or for convenience's sake, as we'll learn in a few chapters.

Step 4: Be consistent. Consistently maintaining our cars (*before* they break down and need expensive repairs) is our most important ♪#shecanic duty.

Step 5: Be a good listener. Poor communication is the number one relationship killer—and the same goes for your relationship with your car. You hang out in your car more days than not, and sometimes for hours. You *know* when something feels, sounds, smells, or looks unusual. That's your car talking to you, telling you something is wrong. Don't ignore your car when it's communicating, whether by speaking to you directly (through the dashboard) or by making unusual noises, emitting suspicious odors, or noticeably vibrating.

Name Your Baby

One last thing: Take pride in your car. For me, that means giving my ride a name, and I suggest you do the same. Call him or her Kimye, Risky Business, the Death Star, or whatever your heart desires. Take a selfie together, and post it with the hashtag #shecanic. The two of you are in this together now—and Kimye or Little Devil is a member of the family.

Must-Know Facts About Your Car

'm currently driving a black 2010 VW Jetta 2.5-liter engine with front-wheel drive. What about you?

If you came up with only the first part of that description, congratulations on being a totally normal human being! Along with factoids like the VIN (vehicle identification number), which travels with your car, this isn't information most people know off the tops of their heads. But it *is* information that you should gather up in one place—the handy form I've included at the end of this chapter. Having this info at your fingertips will help you keep track of what needs to happen with your car—and it'll make calls and conversations with mechanics and customer service reps go a whole lot smoother, too. Here goes!

> **The Year, Make, and Model of Your Car.** You got this! Seems like a no-brainer, but you'd be surprised by how many people are confused about the year their car was made, or don't know whether the model is an L or an LS or a Sport. This information is important, because it will affect what types of fluids, parts, and accessories your mechanic needs to use.

Even being just a year off can mess things up, since parts can change significantly from year to year. You can find it in your owner's manual or by looking up your VIN online on a VIN decoder website (see below).

Your VIN (Vehicle Identification Number). The VIN is your car's fingerprint, a unique seventeen-character serial number that includes numbers and letters and identifies the car's manufacture date and place, along with its make, model, engine size, serial number, and more. The VIN stays with a car throughout its life, even if the car changes hands. You do not need to memorize this number, but you must know where to find it. It is listed on stickers affixed to the driver's-side doorjamb and on the lower left corner of your dashboard. Note: To prevent confusion, VINs don't include the letters O or I; any 0s or 1s are the numbers zero and one.

Your Operating Tire Pressure. Some drivers aren't even aware that they're responsible for putting air in their tires. If you're one of them, you're not alone. Proper tire pressure is probably the single most overlooked maintenance item. But ignoring that blinking dashboard light will make you more likely to get a flat or a sudden blowout and will decrease the life span of your tires. Tires are expensive to replace and essential to the control of your car, so they should be treated like a nice pair of heels.

You'll learn about how to put air in your tires (it's super easy and important) on page 193. The hitch is that every car model has a specific optimal tire pressure—and sometimes it's different for front and rear tires. The operating tire pressure psi (pounds per square inch, the standard unit for measuring air pressure) for your car's particular tires should be listed on a sticker affixed to the driver's-side doorjamb as well as in your owner's manual, but in a pinch the average for a standard passenger car is 33 psi. Note: Operating psi is not the same thing as the maximum pressure listed on the outside of the tire. Overinflated tires will be more vulnerable to damage and less forgiving to potholes.

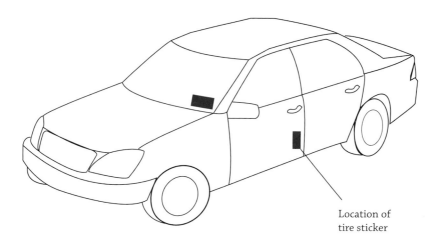

Location of tire sticker

Your Engine Size. Want to really impress someone who knows about cars? Tell him or her the size of your engine. Yeah, baby! How many liters *you* got?

The size of your engine isn't measured by how much oil your engine can hold (typically five quarts) or how many cylinders it contains (whether it's a V-6 or a V-8). Instead, we go by the number of liters of fuel and air its cylinders can hold. I currently drive a 2.5-liter Volkswagen Jetta, which means my engine's cylinders can hold and displace 2.5 liters of fuel and air at a time. Kind of amazing that that's all it takes to get my little car to move.

The bigger the engine, the more power you will have. But with great power comes great responsibility, and a bigger engine will require more oil and gas.

To find out your engine size, look up your car's VIN on a VIN decoder website. Since the VIN is the car's fingerprint, plugging it in online can give you all sorts of information about your car.

Your Drive. Do you have front-wheel drive (FWD), rear-wheel drive (RWD), four-wheel drive (4WD), or all-wheel drive (AWD)? You may not give this much thought once you've made it out of the dealership, but the question will come up during typical maintenance and repair. In a FWD or RWD vehicle, the transmission turns only either the front wheels or the rear wheels. The powertrains of 4WD and AWD vehicles are more expensive at purchase, and because they require more service, they are also more costly to maintain.

Your Maintenance Schedule. I get a lot of questions about maintenance schedules on the GAC Facebook page and in my workshops. How often should you change your oil, replace your air filter, and rotate your tires? You'll find generalized answers on page 56 and in the maintenance and repair charts throughout this book, but the truth is that you'll find the very best recommendations in the owner's manual (sometimes it's a separate booklet) that should have come with your car. Every car has an individual maintenance schedule that will optimize that model's performance, longevity, and health. A 2014 Chevy Cruze has a different schedule than a 2007 Toyota Corolla. Your schedule will tell you things like when to change your oil, when to check your fluids, and when to rotate your tires. Best of all, knowing your maintenance schedule won't just help you take care of your car— it will also help you save money. We'll learn more about how in a bit.

FAST FACTS ABOUT MY CAR

*Jot all your need-to-know info down on this handy page
to make conversations with your mechanic a snap.*

My Vehicle's Year, Make, and Model:

_____

(e.g., 2014 Fiat 500 Sport)

My Vehicle's VIN (vehicle identification number):

_____

(unique seventeen-digit code)

My Vehicle's Engine Size:

_____

(e.g., 2.5 liter)

My Vehicle's Engine Oil Weight:

_____

*(found in owner's manual and often on engine oil cap; e.g.,
10W-30, 5W-20, 5W-30)*

My Vehicle's Transmission System:

_____

(e.g., AWD, 4WD, RWD, FWD)

My Vehicle's Tire Pressure:
Front wheels:_____
Rear wheels:_____
(e.g., 33 psi—see owner's manual or sticker on driver's-side doorjamb)

My Vehicle's Radio Code:

_____

(antitheft code found on some car stereos; see owner's manual)

Get to Know Your Dash

Back in horse-and-buggy days, the dashboard was a wooden or leather protective device on the front of a buggy, preventing passengers from getting splattered with mud "dashed up" by the horses' hooves. Since then, the dashboard has evolved from splash protection to high-tech command center. Along with our radios and climate controls, it houses an information console that allows your car to communicate how it's doing and what it needs. And when cars talk, you should listen and respond.

Like the wash-cycle symbols on a clothing tag, the symbols on a dash can seem confusing. But they're actually very simple—and not necessarily signs that anything is seriously wrong. Every vehicle's dashboard symbols will vary, and your owner's manual

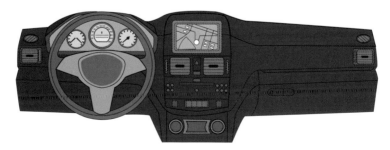

We think of the dash as an electronic console, but the term dashboard *comes from the days when people got around via horse and buggy.*

will list and explain yours. But in this chapter I'm going to give you a quick overview of some of the most common symbols, as well as the instrument cluster that helps you monitor your car's essential functions.

The instrument cluster, featuring the tachometer (left), the speedometer (center), and the fuel and coolant temperature gauges (right). (Placement may vary.)

The Instrument Cluster

Located right behind your steering wheel, the instrument cluster communicates vital information about speed, mileage, gas and oil levels, and engine function. It is composed of the following gauges:

Tachometer. The tachometer measures how fast the parts inside your engine are rotating, using the unit called rpm, or revolutions per minute. The harder you depress the gas pedal, the more revolutions per minute, and the higher the needle on the tachometer climbs. Revolutions per minute above safe operating conditions for an engine are typically indicated by an area of the gauge marked in red. This is where the term *redlining* comes from—revving the engine up past the maximum safe limit. In the redline zone, the engine's internal parts are spinning way too fast, and the engine may become unstable and blow up. For more on the tachometer and why it's important, see "Under the Hood," page 63.

Speedometer. This one's pretty obvious—the speedometer measures how fast the car is going in miles per hour (English or standard) and kilometers per hour (metric).

Odometer. The odometer measures the distance the car has traveled. When your mechanic asks how many miles are on the car, the odometer is where you look.

Fuel Gauge. The fuel gauge measures the gas level in the fuel tank (which is located underneath the backseat). When your fuel is low, a sensor in the fuel tank turns on a switch that illuminates the low-fuel warning light or sends a message to your information center.

Coolant Temperature Gauge. This gauge measures the temperature of the coolant, the fluid that keeps the engine at an optimal temperature. Once the car is warmed up, the needle on the coolant gauge should remain squarely in the center. Do not drive the car if the coolant temperature gauge is running too hot; in some cars, a dashboard light or message center alert will also pop up. For more, see "Under the Hood," page 63.

Battery Voltage and Oil Pressure Gauges. Present in only some cars, these gauges measure battery life and engine oil pressure. In cars *without* such gauges, oilcan and battery symbols will light up on the dash if and when there's an issue. These dashboard lights are both red—because continuing to drive when they are on is a recipe for serious engine damage or even losing all electrical power.

Heating and AC. Most people forget that climate controls are mounted on the dash—and that many of their parts are *inside* the dash.

A Well-Stocked Glove Compartment

Along with being command central for your car, your dashboard contains a storage unit: the glove box, which is a great place to store the following essentials:

- Vehicle registration and insurance information

- Owner's manual

- Flashlight

- Tire pressure gauge

- Pen and small pad of paper

- Repair and maintenance receipts (neatly stashed in an envelope or folded into your owner's manual)

- Emergency and other important phone numbers

- Extra taillights and headlights for quick and easy replacement

- Cell phone charger

- A copy of this book

Mechanics often check for vehicle information inside your glove box, and in the event that you're pulled over or get into a collision, you want to be able to find your registration and insurance info quickly—so it's best to keep your glove box as tidy as possible and clean it up once a year.

Dashboard Lights

Dashboard light symbols are designed to communicate with you about potential problems with your car. So being able to read them is essential.

A close-up of the odometer, where dashboard lights are often clustered; they may also be lined up at the bottom of the instrument cluster (see page 26).

The first thing to know is that dashboard symbols are generally color-coded. This helps you gauge the seriousness of the issue. Here's how it breaks down:

Red light means stop. Red lights indicate serious problems or safety issues that need to be dealt with immediately. Depending on the light, you might be driving yourself to a mechanic immediately or literally pulling over and getting yourself a tow.

Yellow light means slow down. Yellow lights generally indicate issues that should be checked out very soon—but sometimes they just mean that a particular system is activated.

Green or blue light means go. Green or blue lights mean functions are on or activated.

Symbols That Require Immediate Action

A red light doesn't necessarily mean you should panic and trade in your car, but it does require an immediate response.

Brake. First, check to see whether you've inadvertently left your emergency or parking brake on. If not, something is going on with your brakes. You may feel the brake pedal become easier to push and/or drop to the floor. But even if you don't feel anything, pull over and check your brake fluid level (see page 165). If the fluid is very low, call for a tow. If you continue to drive with this light on, you could wind up driving without brakes.

Charging System. This light indicates that your battery is not being charged. Your vehicle is likely to shut off unexpectedly and will probably need to be towed. If this light comes on, get your car to a mechanic immediately.

Oil Pressure. Your oil pressure (*not* the same thing as your oil level) is low. Not having proper oil pressure means oil isn't getting to the engine, which risks causing it serious damage. Shut off your vehicle immediately and check the oil level (see page 111). If your dipstick reads either "low" or "min," add at least 1 quart of oil. Get your vehicle checked out as soon as possible. If you can't get to a mechanic within a five- to ten-minute drive, call for a tow.

Coolant Temperature. *Red:* Your engine temperature is too high. Shut off your vehicle as soon as safely possible and check the coolant level (see page 115). Do not remove the radiator cap while the engine is still hot. If the coolant level is low, add coolant. If your engine continues to overheat, get to a nearby mechanic or call for a tow. *Blue:* Your engine temperature is too low. The most likely cause is a malfunctioning thermostat, and the engine won't run properly until this problem is fixed. Get to a mechanic as soon as you can.

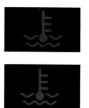

Doors. One or more doors or compartments, including the hood and trunk lid, is not entirely shut.

Power Steering. There is a problem in your power steering system. Get this checked out ASAP. Without power steering, you will not be able to control your car. If you can't get to a mechanic within a five- to ten-minute drive, call for a tow.

Symbols That Will Require Action Soon but Are Not Necessarily Serious

There's no sense in procrastinating when these lights come on, but there's also no cause for alarm.

Check-Engine Light or Maintenance Indicator Light. The check-engine light comes on when your car is burning fuel inefficiently, but it shouldn't be cause for panic. Your engine may be using too much gas or may not be burning the gas properly, causing hazardous pollutants to be released into the environment. A check-engine light can mean there's some kind of complex issue going on, but it can also be the result of something as simple as the gas cap not being screwed on tight enough. It does *not* necessarily always involve the engine itself. It does mean that you'll have to take the vehicle to your mechanic, who will use a computer to scan the onboard diagnostics and retrieve the trouble code, also known as a P code (for powertrain code). This code will help the mechanic diagnose why the vehicle is burning fuel inefficiently.

If the check-engine/maintenance indicator light is flashing, as opposed to steady, you could be causing damage to the engine or to other parts of your car. Shut the vehicle off as soon as safely possible and call for a tow. Do not drive the vehicle with the check-engine light flashing.

Tire Pressure. A handy sensor attached to your tire pressure valve will let you know when tire pressure dips to an unsafe level. The average tire pressure for a passenger vehicle is 33 psi, so this light will come on when one or more tires clocks in at around 28 psi or lower. This symbol will remain lit until the tire is filled.

This light will not come on if the tire pressure is too high, so it's up to you to make sure that you aren't putting too much air in your tires when you fill them. Another thing to note is that dramatic changes in outside temperature will cause pressure in your tires to drop. If you suspect that's the case but the symbol remains lit after you have driven your vehicle for a few miles, get to a gas or service station and try adding air.

If this light is flashing, as opposed to steady, one of the sensors that measures tire pressure is malfunctioning.

Antilock Brakes System (ABS). Antilock brakes  are safety features that prevent one or more of your wheels from locking up, causing your vehicle to slide when you brake. If ABS is compromised, your brakes should still work normally under most conditions. If you do not choose to get this fixed right away, be extra-careful when driving in rain, ice, or snow. To learn all about ABS, see page 162.

If the ABS and ESC (see below) lights come on simultaneously, have the car checked ASAP for a potential safety issue.

Electronic Stability Control (ESC). This function, which can also be labeled VSC (vehicle stability control), helps prevent cars, particularly SUVs, from spinning out or flipping over when driving on winding roads or making sharp turns. A slash through the symbol means the system is not functioning at all.

Air Bags. SRS stands for supplemental restraint system—which is just a fancy term for air bag. When illuminated, this symbol means that one or more air bags is not working and will not activate during an accident. Air bag replacement can be an expensive repair, so how urgently you treat this indicator depends on your personal tolerance for risk.

Parking or Emergency Brake. This light will come on while the parking brake is engaged, and stay lit until that brake is released. If this light is illuminated along with the brake light and your parking brake is not engaged, it is an indication of a brake system failure, which needs immediate attention.

Seat Belts. Someone isn't wearing their seat belt. (This symbol is generally accompanied by a loud beeping.)

Maintenance or Service. An oil change or maintenance-required light means you need an oil change, along with other possible routine maintenance items, depending on how many miles the car has been driven. **Note: This light should be reset after the service is performed.**

Low Fuel/Gas. When this light comes on, it's time to fill up. Always keep your gas above a quarter tank or you could burn out the fuel pump (see page 83).

Cruise Control. This light indicates that your vehicle's cruise control is activated.

Lights. *Yellow:* A headlight is out.
Green or Blue: Headlights, high beams, or fog lights are on, or automatic headlights (present only on some cars) are engaged and will respond to light conditions without you needing to turn them on or off.

Your Primary Care Technician

Most of us see a PCP (primary care physician) for our annual checkup instead of hopping around from doctor to doctor. And we should do the same for our cars, twice a year and whenever they need care. After all, technicians are the auto doctors. But one of the biggest mistakes car owners make is jumping around from mechanic to mechanic in hopes of finding the lowest price or the most convenient location—or, worse, the diagnosis they want to hear. Bad idea. Shop-hopping will make it hard for you to gauge your car's health and to track your service and repair history . . . and leave you more likely to make bad decisions or fall into the clutches of a poorly trained mechanic. The kind of mechanic who may save you money in the short term but will wind up costing you *lots* more in the future.

A car has thousands of moving parts, an intricate internal communication system, and a strong frame to support its load. And when any part of that system breaks down, you should put it in the trusted hands of what I call a primary care technician— your PCT.

Don't Wait for an Emergency

Don't wait until puffs of white smoke start coming out from under your hood to figure out where to take your baby. You wouldn't trust your medical care to the random doctor you passed on your way home from work the week you came down with the flu, would you? But that's exactly how many of us treat our cars. Unless you already have a technician you trust, make it a priority to find one before your next scheduled maintenance appointment. You made the multi-thousand-dollar investment to buy your car, so spend some time finding your PCT.

FYI, *technician* is the official term for *mechanic* now, and I'll be using these two words interchangeably throughout this book. When you see the words *auto tech,* think *mechanic,* and vice versa. And even though I refer to your PCT as a single person, you're likely to be dealing with a few different individuals at a shop or dealership. Think of the shop as a doctor's office where you can be seen by several qualified technicians.

How to Find a PCT (Primary Care Technician)

Most people choose their mechanics either through word of mouth or based on location. I'm going to log a strong vote for going with referrals, but not just any referral. Start by asking your female friends which auto mechanics they trust and feel comfortable with. Give a shout on the ♫#shecanic Facebook community, where recommendations are constantly flying back and forth. Or check sites like womenautoknow.com or askpatty.com. The reason I started Girls Auto Clinic was that men have *very* different experiences in the automotive industry than women do. It's worth checking up on your referrals on sites like Yelp, but know that most auto shops don't tend to have many reviews. Reviews can be extremely subjective, so I'm always skeptical unless there are a lot of them.

Does Certification Matter?

You don't have to complete a two-year trade program to work on cars at a repair facility, and some great mechanics learn on the job. But as the technology inside our cars becomes more and more involved, a degree can help school mechanics on some of the latest developments.

Similarly, an ASE (Automative Service Excellence) certification isn't a prerequisite for working on cars, or necessarily an indication of talent. (Many mechanics are great with a wrench, not so good at test taking.) There are eight main certification tests, and passing all eight makes you a "master tech." You have to keep taking the tests every five years to stay current on your certifications, and many independent shops don't keep up with those requirements and/or can't pay master techs the higher wages they demand. But I see certifications as signs that mechanics are committed to staying on top of changing technology, so if you're making the choice between two PCTs and one has a certification, I say go for it—though in my opinion, referrals and good reviews trump ASEs. Most people don't realize it, but you can always ask if a shop hires ASE technicians.

How to Assess a PCT

Most car owners would list service, price, reliability, and quick turn-around as qualities they look for in a mechanic. Let's add communication and respect to that list. Do you feel respected as a customer? Are your cares and concerns acknowledged and addressed? It is your right to expect a level of customer service you feel comfortable with.

To find out if a potential PCT is the right fit for you, use these pointers to assess your comfort level and his or her suitability.

A great PCT should be friendly and patient. He or she should listen to your concerns, clearly communicate a plan for diagnosing, repairing, or servicing your vehicle, and ease any worries you express. You shouldn't feel anxious or worried when talking to your PCT! Phone calls are fine, but I prefer to talk to technicians in person. You'll get a better feel for their personality and for how they interact with their customers. Mechanics can be rough around the edges, and it's important that you feel safe and comfortable with yours. You should never feel disrespected.

A great PCT should be easy to understand. Can the technician explain what's going on with your car in terms you can understand? I believe this is very important. If a PCT cannot explain the diagnosis in a way that makes you feel comfortable with the repair, *run*. Actually, drive. As the saying goes: "If you can't explain it to a five-year-old, you don't understand it well enough."

A great PCT should understand the balance between urgent and nonurgent repairs. He or she shouldn't try to sell you everything under the sun. A PCT's primary concerns should be that your car runs well, you are safe, and you are avoiding expensive repairs later on. A PCT should say things like "Hey, I noticed you have a small oil leak. You will want to keep an eye on it," or "Your tire tread is looking low—save up some money because your tires will need replacing in the next three months." You shouldn't feel pressure to approve any nonurgent repair!

A great PCT can diagnose the root cause(s) of your car's problems—even if it takes some time. Electrical issues and computer problems can be tricky for even the most experienced PCTs to diagnose. But if a PCT is struggling with an issue like a check-engine light or no start, or if you have to bring your car back to the shop after a repair didn't take, you shouldn't be charged for every little thing they do to figure it out. A trustworthy PCT is patient and thorough when diagnosing and repairing a car, and charges you a fair amount for the time and diagnostic work. There *will* be a charge for diagnosing your car for noise, check-engine lights, computer problems, or electrical issues, and the amount will depend on how long the PCT spent on the issue. Some diagnoses take less than ten minutes, while complex problems on newer, highly technical cars can take more than an hour to diagnose. Which is why, as cars become more computerized, it's so important to find a smart PCT who's skilled at diagnostics.

A great PCT should be able to admit faults and limitations. No one is perfect. Sometimes even a very good mechanic will break something or mess up a repair. Just as doctors sometimes make a mistake, so can mechanics. It happens. It doesn't and shouldn't happen often. But when it does, an honest PCT admits to being at fault. Likewise, a trustworthy PCT will let you know beforehand if a particular issue falls outside of his or her realm of expertise and will recommend another business or expert who can help you.

Choosing a Mechanic: Dealerships vs. Chains vs. Indies

If your car is still under warranty with its manufacturer and a few years of "free" maintenance were built into the price of your car, your PCT should be your dealership. If you didn't select a maintenance package with a new car purchase or you drive a used or older car, you'll need to make a decision about where to get your care. Here's a guide to the pros and cons of visiting dealerships; chains like Jiffy Lube, Pep Boys, Firestone, and Meineke; and independent shops.

Dealerships: The Pros

+ If you purchased a maintenance package, regular maintenance visits will be free for your first few years of ownership. (For more on how to read the fine print, see page 270.) Keep in mind that maintenance packages aren't actually free, since they're built into the price of buying the car or priced out separately.

+ Dealerships are staffed by well-trained professionals and generally provide good, consistent customer service.

+ Dealerships offer perks like loaner cars, pick-up and drop-off services, online scheduling, and amenities such as food, fancy coffee machines, kids' play areas, Wi-Fi, lounges, and so on. But there is a con to all these amenities—their price is passed on to you.

+ Dealerships have access to the most up-to-date technology and equipment.

+ Dealerships often offer automated service reminders and other tools to help you keep your maintenance on track.

+ Dealership technicians are highly trained to know your particular make of vehicle inside and out. If you have a European car (see page 262), you will have to go to the dealership for certain repairs.

+ Dealerships use OEM (original equipment manufacturer) parts, as opposed to the "aftermarket" or generic parts you'll get on some repairs from independent shops or chains. If you're at a Ford dealership, you'll be getting a Ford part for a replacement.

+ If you run into trouble with service at a dealership, there will always be someone further up the chain (or far away in a customer service center) for you to call.

+ You'll save yourself the time and trouble of having to research PCTs in your area.

+ Dealerships' waiting rooms will be sparkling clean.

Dealerships: The Cons

- Servicing your car at a dealership is going to cost you—labor and parts are both much more expensive. If your warranty has expired or a repair falls outside your warranty, you'll likely be shelling out two to three times what you'd pay at a chain or an independent shop.

- You're likely to be dealing with a service adviser who doesn't touch or see your car rather than directly with a mechanic— though you should definitely ask to speak directly with whoever worked on your car if you need clarification about something.

- Your service adviser *will* be trained at selling you on parts and services you may not need. Dealerships *love* to upsell customers on everything from hoses and clamps to replacements on half-worn brake pads and rotors, whereas an independent mechanic might tell you to hold off on replacing those brake pads and rotors for another six months. Remember: A great PCT doesn't try to sell you everything under the sun. Many dealerships will, so be empowered and educated.

- Dealership technicians have a depth of knowledge when it comes to your vehicle's make, but they often don't have the breadth of knowledge and experience that comes from exposure to a wide variety of cars. Nor do they have some magic wand that enables them to correctly diagnose a car every time—dealership technicians struggle with complex diagnoses just as much as the next tech!

- Your options may be limited to a single dealership in your area.

- Some dealerships are run by businesspeople who prioritize sales, branding, and publicity over employee training and development, long-term relationships with customers, and quality of service.

- Technicians are paid by the job rather than by the hour. The upside for technicians is they can make more money by being quick and thorough. Really great technicians love this model. The downside? Mechanics aren't incentivized to spend extra time on your car, and even experienced techs can forget or overlook things as they rush.

But It's So Dirty!

Don't be put off by a dirty garage—unless it's accompanied by subpar customer service and a palpable sense of poor organization. This is a dirty job! Some of the best mechanics I know work in filthy but bustling shops. Clean bathrooms, nice waiting rooms, and pristine garages may be appealing, but these customer-facing touches can drive up overhead. Dealerships tend to get an A+ for cleanliness, but they often fail when it comes to customer service and price.

Clean or dirty, sitting around in a waiting room at an auto shop is never going to be high on your list of fun things to do. But as a #shecanic, you recognize that regular visits to your PCT are essential to the health and wellness of your vehicle, right?

The Major Chains: The Pros

+ Convenience and recognition. The major chains are everywhere.

+ Speed and price. If everything is functioning as advertised, service can be very quick and inexpensive.

+ Chains often offer automated service reminders and other tools to help keep your maintenance on track.

+ If you run into trouble with service at a chain, there is likely someone further up the ladder (or far away in a customer service center) for you to call.

+ Waiting areas are generally clean.

+ You *can* make a well-run chain location your PCT, but know that you're not going to get the same service at every location. And turnover rates are high, which means that you might get good service one year and then find that everyone you dealt with has moved on.

The Major Chains: The Cons

- Name-brand recognition may give customers the illusion that chain auto techs are more trustworthy or highly trained, but in fact you'll still need to do your research to find the right location.

- With high turnover rates and lower pay, chains don't necessarily attract the best or most experienced mechanics. Technicians may have received cursory on-the-job training rather than a classroom education or an in-depth mentorship.

- Chains are largely run by businesspeople who prioritize sales, branding, and publicity over employee training and development, customer relationships, and quality of service.

- You're likely to be dealing with a service adviser who doesn't touch or see your car rather than directly with a mechanic— though you should definitely ask to speak directly with whoever worked on your car if you need clarification about something.

- Again, your service adviser *will* be trained at selling you on parts and services you may not need. Chains *love* to upsell customers. Be educated and empowered, #shecanic!

- Chains tend to downprice their oil changes and maintenance items so that they can upsell captive customers.

- Chains use aftermarket parts that are cheaper than OEM parts at dealerships. The quality of those parts varies greatly.

- Chains may rush through jobs in order to service as many cars a day as possible, assembly-line style. This is how mistakes happen and things like adding engine oil or tightening lug nuts get missed.

- Customer service can be inconsistent, varying from location to location.

Parts Stores and Diagnostics

Price-conscious ♪#shecanics, don't waste your time taking your car to a parts store for a free diagnosis. Take it to your PCT!

While some people who work at AutoZone and other parts stores are graduates of automotive technology schools, often the employers and managers are people who understand parts better than they understand auto repair. The main incentive of a parts store is to sell you those parts. Their free check-engine-light troubleshooting consists of giving you a printout of your P codes (see page 131), but P codes are just the first clue as to what is going on. A mechanic still needs to read the codes and diagnose the problem.

Independents: The Pros

+ Independent shops' prices on both parts and labor will be lower than dealership rates and comparable to if not lower than those at the chains.

+ Good independent shops are great at relationships. They will give you the hands-on treatment that leaves a ♫#shecanic feeling secure and understood.

+ There may be low turnover among staff, and owners and staff are often members of your community. At a really great indie shop, you'll feel like family.

+ Indie mechanics may be able to give extra care and time to your car if they're being paid a salary instead of being paid per job.

+ Independents may reward returning customers with discounts or free line items such as tire rotations—like getting that tenth pedicure for free. Independents live and die by referrals, so smart shop owners are invested in keeping their customers happy.

+ Independent auto techs may be open to negotiating on price. Mechanics don't tend to negotiate on repairs under $500, but they might be able to give you a break on a very labor-intensive, expensive repair.

+ Indies often offer shuttle service to and from work or your home.

+ Some indie shops have waiting areas that are on par with, if not better than, dealerships'.

+ Trustworthy independent shops won't upsell you on repairs or parts, because they're more interested in keeping you as a return customer than in making a onetime sale.

Independents: The Cons

- Independent shops may lack the up-to-date technology and equipment or the highly trained technicians to work on newer, luxury, specialty, or foreign cars—unless they specialize in these types of cars.

- Smaller independent shops may take longer to perform service or repairs on your car if they don't have the staff.

- Quality and service will vary drastically from one independent shop to another. You'll need to do your research!

- Independent shops use aftermarket parts that are cheaper than the OEM parts used at dealerships. The quality of these parts will vary greatly.

- Small mom-and-pop shops tend to have small waiting rooms that can sometimes be dingy, dusty, and uncomfortable.

Work That Body (Shop)

Though they're frequently confused, *auto body shops* and *auto repair shops* are two diffcrent animals. An auto repair shop, aka a garage, is the place where you take your car for internal maintenance and repair. An auto body shop or collision repair center specializes in expensive repair work on the outside, or body, of your car. That's where you want to go after you get in a crash or someone scratches your paint job with a key.

Talking to Your PCT

As a mechanic, I've definitely seen women come into the automotive sphere with their guard up, assuming they're going to get ripped off or talked down to. If that rings a bell with you, take a deep breath and hit the reset button.

A great PCT should be easy to talk to, but the following tips will help you comfortably assert yourself as a confident ♪#shecanic and an excellent customer.

Never be embarrassed to ask questions. I always tell attendees of my Girls Auto Clinic workshops they should *never* feel embarrassed or ashamed to ask questions. Educating yourself is something you should feel proud of! And this should apply to all of your interactions with your friendly PCT.

Ask to be shown the issue on your car. If you don't understand your mechanic's explanation of the diagnosis or the fix, ask him or her to show you on your car. Some issues won't be visible, but most failures on cars can be seen, heard, smelled, or felt. And if a mechanic can see it, hear it, smell it, or feel it, so can you! Use statements like "I want to hear what you're hearing." If your discussion takes place over the phone, ask your mechanic to save your old parts so that he or she can help explain the diagnosis when you come to pick up the car.

Ask for an estimate of the cost. You probably won't need to ask—no mechanic *should* perform a job without first giving you an estimate, either verbal or written. They need your approval to proceed with the repair.

Ask what you need to do now, and what can be saved for later. If you're facing a steep repair bill and your mechanic hasn't automatically offered up the information already, ask if any of the line items could be safely saved for later. A good mechanic will be honest with you about what's truly necessary and what could be put off for another six months. Especially on an older car with a limited life span, it may not be worth your while to repair everything right away.

Don't take it out on your mechanic! Car problems can be a real bummer. You're innocently going about your business, and all of a sudden your check-engine light comes on. Next thing you know your mechanic is telling you that you'd better forget about that vacation you were planning—you're gonna be out $1,200. But cars are unpredictable. Parts will break, and systems will fail. This is true of anything that is engineered by human beings, from static buildings to machines filled with moving parts. Any part or system that exerts energy and power will eventually fail or die. And if the failure is a result of your negligence, all the more reason not to take it out on your innocent mechanic. Breathe, take a moment, and read on to find out more about how mechanics price their jobs.

How Repair Shops Price Their Jobs

If your mechanic hands you a bill that seems totally mysterious, you're not alone. Given the many different types of jobs, the many different types of cars on the market, and the fluctuating costs of parts, prices for repairs (unlike maintenance tasks) can be tough to predict.

I've estimated the price range for common maintenance jobs on page 56, and you'll find mentions of price ranges for specific jobs throughout this book. The price of repairs, especially major ones, is another story. To get a sense of why they vary so much, let's take a look at how auto repair shops set their prices. Generally, their prices are based on 1) a diagnostic fee, 2) the hourly labor rate for performing the repair, 3) the cost of any replacement parts, and 4) fees.

1. Diagnostic Fee. When you car comes in for any issue, the technician's first step is diagnosing the problem before recommending a repair. This can take anywhere from thirty minutes to two or more hours, and you will be charged a diagnostic fee for this time—unless a diagnosis takes less than fifteen minutes, in which case most shops won't charge you a separate fee (provided you get the repair performed at their shop).

2. Hourly labor rate. After the car has been diagnosed and a repair has been recommended, each shop has an hourly charge for labor. (Dealerships have the highest labor rates, starting at around $100 per hour and going up to $150 per hour or more.) You will be charged the labor rate times the amount of hours it takes to repair your car, based on an industry standard.

3. Parts. All independent repair shops and chains make money off parts by buying them at wholesale prices, then reselling them to you at retail prices; there's less variation at dealerships, since they're almost always using OEM (original manufacturer equipment) parts—the most expensive parts. But you're still not better off buying parts yourself and bringing them to your independent PCT. You *might* get a better deal on a quality part by shopping around—or you might get a cheaper part that will fail in six months. Aftermarket automotive parts are a billion-dollar industry, with parts made everywhere from China to India to the United States. Quality fluctuates greatly, and shops game the market by getting their parts from multiple manufacturers and distributors. So it's best not to play around unless you know what you're doing. Leave it to your PCT to buy quality parts for a fair price.

4. Repair shops often charge a small shop fee to cover the cost of supplies and disposal of old parts and fluids. Things like rags, wheel weights, brake grease, oil disposal, tire recycling, and so on will be included in either a flat rate or an added percentage to your bill.

Mobile Mechanics: Legit or Shady?

A mechanic who comes to your house and fixes your car right there in your driveway sounds like a pretty good deal, right? Mobile mechanics are great for things like oil changes and brakes, but they are limited when it comes to repairs and diagnoses because they won't have all the tools and equipment required to work on a car. Environmental regulations may restrict mobile mechanics as well. There are exceptions, and a few startups are trying to innovate in this space, but as a general rule I wouldn't advise going with a mobile mechanic unless you've done the research to make sure you're dealing with someone legit.

Should You Haggle?

A small study showed that independent repair shops may be willing to lower prices if you ask, and even dealerships *can* sometimes lower their rates. A mechanic may give you a lower price as a first-time customer to get you to come back again (though this isn't something you'd ask for) on a repair over $500. But good mechanics price their jobs fairly from the start, so I personally wouldn't recommend haggling.

Just Say *No* to Those Chicken Nuggets!

Ladies, I like the occasional Happy Meal as much as the next #shecanic. But when it comes to oil changes or brake repairs, just say no to those chicken nuggets. Those golden arches may tempt us with the promise of a delightful four-nugget snack for only $1.99. But you gotta ask—what else is in those nuggets that they can afford to price them at less than fifty cents a pop? It ain't 100% chicken, that's for sure.

That's the way I feel about oil changes for $19.95 or fifty-dollar brake jobs. These chicken nuggets of the auto repair industry are really enticements to get customers in the door, at which point you are slammed over the head with a bunch of stuff you probably don't need. Shops that operate this way may use low-quality oil or parts, or even forget to change the oil in their rush to get through the job. And they certainly won't be looking over your car to spot any potential issues like a quality PCT should. Even for something as simple as an oil change, don't give in to the lure of the nugget.

As far as shopping around for lower prices on repairs, that's an approach I just can't recommend. You'll always be able to find someone who's willing to do a cheaper job, but at what price to your car? Trust me, the odds are pretty good that you're going to find yourself paying for it later. The lowest price probably means low-quality parts and an inexperienced or rushed technician. I've definitely seen how trying to pinch pennies in the area of auto repair can come back to haunt people. At best, the repair or service will need to be repeated at your expense. At worst, the repair or service could damage an expensive component of your vehicle, like the transmission.

High Maintenance

Now it's time to talk about how often you should be visiting your mechanic: Showing up for scheduled maintenance appointments (generally every six months) is vital to the health of your car. As for what goes on during those visits, most of us seriously underestimate how much maintenance a car needs. Especially when it comes to newer rides, we assume oil changes and tire rotations will be the extent of the damage. That may be true for the first couple of years, but a car is a large and complex mechanical instrument filled with moving parts. We're talking thousands of pounds of steel, aluminum, plastic, and glass, with joints, pulleys, pumps, and gears that rust and wear down as they rub up against each other and degrade over time. Until that self-driving car of the future comes with self-regenerating parts, we're going to be maintaining our rides.

The idea of spending money and time now, for no other reason than avoiding having to spend more money and more time later, isn't sexy. But most things we value need to be maintained.

Your Wheels, Your $$$: Some Preventative Maintenance Is Free

What is preventative maintenance? The ongoing habit of preserving and restoring your car so it (a) lasts as long as possible, and (b) doesn't break down on you in the middle of rush hour. The good news is that anytime you bring your car into a repair center, your technician is going to be giving you a bit of free preventative maintenance by doing a quick checkup. For the price of that repair—even for just a simple oil change—you're also getting a little freebie. Some technicians will go into more detail than others, but every technician should be performing a minimum health check: looking for, listening to, and feeling for any abnormal issues.

Another win for maintenance: Prices on maintenance line items are much more predictable than they are for repairs, which can involve lots of diagnosing and sometimes a few dead ends. For more on budgeting for maintenance and repairs, see the timetable starting on page 56.

A Master Schedule

In every car's owner's manual, there is a detailed timetable of maintenance tasks. This is your maintenance schedule, and it's specific to your car's make and model. My 2010 VW Jetta has a different maintenance schedule than a 2008 Chevy Impala or a 2014 Kia Sorento.

Knowing your car's particular maintenance schedule will help you do two things:

1. Properly maintain your vehicle.

2. Avoid shelling out cold hard cash for upsells you don't need. (They can't sell you an air filter every time you go in for an oil change if you know how often you really need a new one.)

One of the most important auto maintenance tasks happens to be one of the cheapest and simplest: getting your oil changed regularly and promptly. It's so important that I'm gonna say it again. *Getting your oil changed promptly when it is due is the single most important thing you can do for your car.* But there are also other parts of your car that must be maintained.

If you can't find your maintenance schedule in your owner's manual (or you can't find your owner's manual), do an online search for the owner's manual for the year, make, and model of your car, and then print it out, or download it and save a baby tree.

Maintenance charts can be confusing, so take some time with yours. I've provided some basic rules of thumb in this chapter, but your particular chart should still be your primary guide.

In general, cars require some form of maintenance at least every six months. Many charts break tasks down in miles, but most of us don't think in miles and aren't in the habit of tracking our mileage. So I use months in my timetables—though if you're someone who drives a lot, mileage will be a better cue. If you're using months, go ahead and enter a recurring biannual reminder into your digital calendar. Between your dash, the dated sticker your PCT will put on your windshield after a service appointment, and your automated reminders, you'll be sure to get the message.

THE BASIC TIMETABLES

ITEM	CHECK	SERVICE	PRICE
Engine Oil	Every month for cars with over 50,000 miles; every gas fill-up for cars with over 100,000 miles	Every 3–6 months	$35–$80, depending on oil type and engine size
Other Essential Fluids	Every oil change or every 6 months	Varies, as recommended by your owner's manual	$60–$150, depending on fluid type. Oil is inexpensive compared to transmission fluid
Hoses and Drive Belts	Every year for rotting, cracks, and flexibility	As needed, but usually within 5 years	$100 or less
Battery	Every oil change check for corrosion	Lasts 4–5 years	$150 or less
Air Filter	Every oil change	Every 1–2 years	$40 or less for most cars

ITEM	CHECK	SERVICE	PRICE
Tires	Check for tread wear and rotting every month; rotate tires once a year	If you rotate tires every year and maintain tire pressure and alignment angles, tires can last 5 years or more	$95 and up per tire on smaller cars, $150 and up per tire on larger cars
Brakes	Every oil change check for wear and leaks	Average is 2–3 years for disc, 5 years for drums; really depends on how you drive	$150–$400 per axle (front or rear)
Steering Parts	Every year check for looseness, wear, and leaks	As needed; normally start to wear after 80,000 miles	Varies greatly
Suspension Parts	Every year check for looseness, wear, and leaks	As needed; normally start to wear after 80,000 miles	Varies greatly
Wipers	Every oil change check for wear and tear	As needed	$15–$30
Lights	Every oil change check for blown lights	As needed	Varies from $10 to $150, depending on car design

ITEM	CHECK	SERVICE	PRICE
Timing Belt	n/a	100,000 miles	More than $650
Car Wash, Wax, Vac	n/a	Every 3 months; wash undercarriage after every snowstorm	$15–$50 for a quick wash or DIY; $100–$200 for detail

Is It a Tune-up or a Checkup?

A *checkup* is a simple check on your car's vital signs. Like a doctor, your PCT will check over your car and recommend any necessary repairs or service. This involves a test drive, during which your PCT will listen and feel for any issues with your engine, transmission, brakes, and suspension. Next, your PCT will put the car on a lift and check the undercarriage for issues such as fluid leaks, suspension damage, steering damage, tire wear, or brake wear. Last, your PCT will check all fluids and filters. All of this costs only $35, and should be done once a year or before a long road trip.

A *tune-up* happens around 80,000 to 100,000 miles. It requires replacing spark plugs and any of the following if needed: wires and coils, fuel and air filters, and the PCV valve. The cost should be anywhere from $250 to $500. If your car is in dire need of a tune-up, the check-engine light will illuminate.

Don't Forget to Wash Your Car!

If you're like me, car washes happen to your car every time it rains. But seriously, it's important to keep up with regular cleanings if you want your car to last—and to fetch the highest possible resale price. Just like our clothes, our cars need to be properly laundered in order to attain optimal longevity. It's a good idea to give your car a thorough cleaning (inside, outside, and underneath) at least once a year, ideally twice. If you get snow where you live, you'll want to wash your car and its undercarriage as soon as the winter season is over, as well as every two weeks during frequent snowy conditions; if you get infrequent or light snow, within five days of snowfall.

Salt sprinkled on roads to melt ice and snow during winter creates safer driving conditions, but it also causes rust or corrosion on your car as it is kicked up from the road and sticks to the car's undercarriage and body. As salt builds up, it will rust frames, metal brake lines, suspension parts, bolts, and more. This *will* cause expensive repairs as your car ages and/or decrease the resale price, so prevent rust and corrosion damage by regularly washing your car during winter months at an establishment that offers undercar, undercarriage, or underspray services.

Normal Use vs. Severe Use

There are two types of "use" patterns for your car or motor vehicle—regular or normal use and severe or harsh use. Your owner's manual will recommend maintenance intervals based on which one you fall under. Severe use can involve towing, hauling, and a lot of stop-and-go traffic. Most of us belong in the normal category, but the chart on the following page explains the difference. One thing that might surprise you is that short trips are actually harder on a car than long ones—so if you mostly use your car to run errands in your neighborhood, you may fall under the severe use category.

NORMAL USE	SEVERE USE
Most trips over 10 miles	Most trips fewer than 4 to 10 miles
Driving in temperatures *above* freezing (32°F)	Driving in temperatures *below* freezing (32°F)
Most trips are not stop and go	Most trips are stop and go
No towing or carrying heavy loads	Towing or carrying heavy loads
Driving on roads or conditions that are not dusty	Driving on dusty roads or in dusty conditions
Car has fewer than 100,000 miles on it	Car has more than 100,000 miles on it

Maintenance and Your Dashboard

Listen up, your car is talking.

Remember those dashboard lights we learned all about a couple of chapters ago? Modern cars are outfitted with dedicated dashboard lights and sometimes even message centers that will let you know when maintenance is needed. Based on the manufacturer's recommended mileage benchmarks, the signal will usually tell you that general maintenance is required but won't  get specific about what kind of maintenance that might be. A symbol may simply become illuminated, or you could get a message like "change oil now" or "maintenance due." If you want to get a sense of what you're in for, check your owner's manual to see what maintenance is recommended at your current mileage milestone.

Oil Life Monitors

Some cars come equipped with oil life monitors that give specific feedback about the state of your oil. These work several ways:

1. By tracking the vehicle's miles. As you get closer to the number of miles required for an oil change, a "change oil" message or symbol on the dash will light up. This mileage amount corresponds to the recommendations in your owner's manual.

2. By electronically tracking the efficiency of the oil over time, measuring miles driven, the number of times the engine was started, and other determining factors. Highway miles are easier on oil than shorter city drives, so the number of times you start an engine or drive in stop-and-go traffic will significantly affect the condition of your oil.

3. By measuring the oil's acidity, contaminants, and viscosity via a sensor (usually a luxury feature).

On most cars, maintenance and/or oil change lights will need to be manually reset after maintenance is performed—something auto techs may forget to do. Without a reset, many oil life monitors won't give accurate readings. So make sure yours has gone dark again before you leave the shop. Or check your owner's manual, or google "maintenance reset" for the year, make, and model of your car for directions on how to reset the light yourself. On some cars, it's done via a button on the dash. On others, it's a complicated maneuver, like pumping the brakes five times with the ignition off.

Your Wheels, Your $$$: Don't Procrastinate!

The golden rule of maintenance? *Don't put it off.* That applies double to the most important maintenance item on the list: the oil change, which also happens to be the most frequent maintenance task of all. If your maintenance schedule recommends an oil change every 5,000 miles, that doesn't mean take your car in at 5,001 miles or 5,482 miles. Take care of business at mile 4,999 or before. Why? Frequently checking up on your car's health is the only way to predict and affect its long-term behavior. If you're tired of high-priced, unexpected repairs that can financially set you back months or years and create added stress in your life, you must change the way you view car maintenance. Discipline equals freedom. Do you pay less now or pay more later? A ♪#shecanic knows the answer. So get in the habit of prompt oil changes. Unless you like to blow your cash.

I'd rather spend mine on tacos and margaritas.

DIY #1: Under the Hood

My childhood fear of peeking under the bed turned into an adult pattern of avoidance—as an auto airhead I acted like there really *were* monsters lurking under my hood. I just knew the car monsters were going to get me and my wallet. And anytime something wasn't quite right, I was afraid to lift the hood.

But now we're going to pop the latch, get the lay of the land, and confront those icky monsters once and for all. We'll learn which parts are safe to touch and work on ourselves, and which ones we can monitor but should outsource to a professional. We'll locate the reservoirs that sometimes get thirsty for oil and fluids. Then, later on, we'll put that knowledge into action by tackling a few simple DIY techniques that every driver should be able to conquer.

All of this learning comes with one simple condition: Instead of just following along, I want you to grab a rag and some gloves, bring this book out to your car—and then actually, physically open up your hood and take a look at what's going on under there.

Yup. Things are about to get just a little bit dirty.

That maze of dirt, grease, metal parts, wires, and hoses is going to make a lot more sense once we've gotten through this. Let's get ready to shine a light onto that scary dark spot full of vehicular monsters. (Spoiler alert: They're not so scary after all.)

Pop That Hood

More often than not, the women who attend my Girls Auto Clinic workshops share a dirty little secret: They don't know how to open the hoods of their cars. Do you?

Like I said, there's no place for shame in my workshops. So what we're going to do now is start at the very beginning.

The hood of a modern car can be opened and propped by various means, but there are usually three steps involved: pulling a cable to pop the hood, releasing the hood from the safety catch, and propping the hood open. The only tricky part is locating the various parts involved. If you're still having a hard time, check your owner's manual or ask your PCT to show you next time you're at the shop.

> 1. Pop the hood. Designated by a symbol of a car with its hood open or the word *hood,* a lever inside your car that's attached to the hood latch cable will be your first stop. The lever will most commonly be found on the driver's side, by your left leg or foot, but it may also be on the steering column or under the steering wheel—or, much more rarely, on the front of the car. Grab the lever and pull it hard, and your hood will pop up slightly.

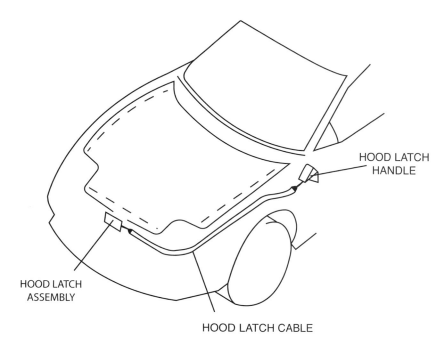

HOOD LATCH
HANDLE

HOOD LATCH
ASSEMBLY

HOOD LATCH CABLE

*Find the latch commonly located by the driver's
left foot to unlock your hood.*

2. Release the hood. At this point the hood will be popped
but still locked. To open or raise it, you'll have to release
the hood from a latch on the front of the car, and finding the
latch may take some doing. Look and feel for it under the
still-closed, popped hood by getting down to eye level.
The latch should be located right in the center of the hood,
and usually needs to be pushed up or to the left to unlatch.

3. Prop the hood. Once you've released the hood from its
latch, you'll be able to raise it. Because the hood is heavy,
it will also need to be propped to stay open, via either a
hydraulic strut (i.e., a self-propping mechanism) or a prop
rod. (See dotted red lines on image, above, for possible
locations.)

If your hood doesn't stay propped on its own, look around for a metal rod under the hood, near the latch, on the underside of the hood, or off to the side. Stick the rod into a hole on the bottom or belly of the hood. (The spot might be marked by an arrow.) Make sure the hood is securely propped before getting to work. Again, consult your owner's manual for instructions on propping it open safely. Or better yet, find a video online!

A Note on Directions

To avoid confusion when working on cars, mechanics use the perspective of a seated driver to describe the location of a part or issue. So though a part may be to the left from the perspective of a PCT standing at the front of the car and working on that part under the hood, they will refer to the part as being to the right. When you're describing a problem to your PCT, you'll always refer to the part from the perspective of a seated driver—e.g., "right front tire" means the front tire on the passenger side.

But to keep things simple as we take our tour under the hood, I've described the location of parts from the perspective of a person facing the front of the car.

The Monsters Under the Hood

We'll be taking a detailed monster tour in a bit, but here's a quick breakdown of the four major categories of stuff you'll find under your hood:

Your Car's Essential Fluids. With the exception of gas, which is held in the back of the car, all of your car's essential fluids—engine oil, coolant, transmission fluid, power steering fluid, brake fluid, and window washing fluid.

Your Car's Electrical Center. The battery, starter, and alternator—the parts that get the car up and running and then feed the car's electrical components.

The Engine and Her Friends. The workhorse at the center of it all, along with the accessories that help her do her job— think air filter, dipstick, oil filler cap, spark plugs, radiator, and belts.

The AC System. We aren't going to talk much about the AC system, since it doesn't require maintenance, aside from occasional repairs.

In luxury vehicles, you'll often see a hard-shell plastic covering protecting most of the parts under the hood from dirt and mois-ture. If that's the case for you, you won't be able to see the engine or most related parts without removing this cover, but you'll still be able to add fluids and check certain parts for wear and tear—both of which we're going to learn to do later in this book.

A Tour of the Essential Fluids Under the Hood

If you've popped open your hood, you're already farther into the monster zone than some car owners ever venture. Nice work, ♪#shecanic. Now let's take a look at the reservoirs that store your car's essential fluids. Follow along on the diagram and through this section to locate them on your car. The engine, radiator, and brake fluid placement are invariable, but the rest of the parts pictured will move around depending on the make and model. Essential fluids often have identifying labels on the their caps; I've also designated each part with a *touch* or *don't touch* icon to help keep you safe. Now let's get ready to get our hands dirty.

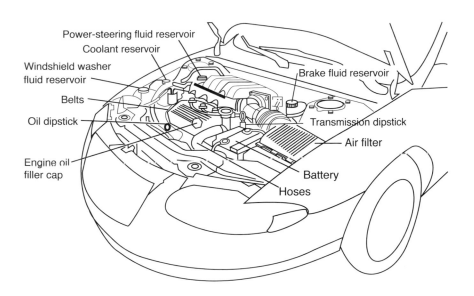

The master plan—a look at what's going on under the hood.

Engine Oil. Remember, oil is your vehicle's lifeline. Would you prefer to spend $5 on a quart of oil, or $3,000 to replace your engine?

Thought so.

Located front and center under the hood, the engine sits over the oil pan—where engine oil is stored. We pour oil into the engine by unscrewing the oil filler cap located right on top of the engine and typically marked with an oilcan symbol or words identifying the type of oil. See instructions on how to check and refill your oil on page 109.

Power Steering Fluid. Normally sitting to the left of the engine, the power steering reservoir is filled with a reddish or pinkish fluid that turns dark brown over time—a signal that the system is in need of a flush. Not a DIY but a task for your PCT, a flush should take place every three to five years, or as recommended by your owner's manual. Checking your power steering fluid level yourself, however, is totally doable, and we'll learn how on page 173. It's a good idea to check your fluid level before any trip longer than two hours, or as needed when you suspect a steering issue. Signs include grinding noises while turning the steering wheel, or a steering wheel that feels tighter or looser than normal.

Coolant. Despite its name, the coolant under your hood is pressurized—which makes it hotter than other fluids. Hot enough to cause severe burns. To add coolant or check your coolant level safely, see page 116 for instructions on how to check and refill. A mix of antifreeze and water (70/30 or 50/50), the neon fluid comes in bright colors like orange, pink, or green, and it's just as important to the engine function as the oil we've discussed time and time again.

Brake Fluid. On standard vehicles, brake fluid is usually located in the same place— directly behind the steering wheel. On hybrid vehicles, it tends to be on the passenger side. White wine in color when new and dark brown when past its prime, the fluid goes through extreme ranges of temperature while in use—at times reaching 400 degrees Fahrenheit. The brake system is a closed system, meaning that fluid is not supposed to be topped off when low. Low brake fluid is an indication that either something is wrong with your brakes or you need to replace your brake pads. For instructions on how to check your brake fluid level, see page 173.

Windshield Washer Fluid. The windshield washer fluid reservoir holds the blue stuff that helps us wipe our windshields free from dirt, snow, bugs, and bird dung. Despite what you may have heard, making homemade washer fluid or substituting dish soap is not a great idea. The store-bought stuff can contain chemicals that won't freeze in the winter or be specially formulated to help dissolve summertime's bug and pollen deposits. The summertime washer fluids (also known as bug and tar fluids) may freeze in winter, so make sure you change them out before then. And please don't attempt to use your wipers to deice your windshield! A ♩#shecanic uses a proper ice scraper to remove ice and snow from her windshield.

Fluid Flushes

Back in my auto airhead days, I thought a fluid flush was an easy way for a shop to get me to spend money on something my car didn't really need. But in fact, where applicable, it's an inexpensive way to maintain expensive equipment.

After going through cycles of drastic temperature changes and picking up metal particles as they travel through our car's systems, our fluids need to be replaced. The systems themselves can be prone to sludge and particle buildup, so in some cases just changing the fluid isn't enough. That's where flushes come into the picture, using a chemical detergent to clean the fluid pathways of the sludge and buildup—think cleaning your teeth of plaque or adding vinegar to the dishwasher to remove scum deposits.

Checking and topping off your fluid flushes is something you will learn to do in this book, but flushing and draining fluids can be done only by a PCT. (*Drain and refill* means you're skipping a chemical flush.) Read on to find out which fluids require a flush, and how often.

Transmission Fluid. Transmission fluid is not maintained often, but on some cars the transmission system must be flushed after a certain number of miles, with the transmission filter simultaneously replaced. Check your owner's manual or talk with your PCT to see if this applies to you.

Engine Oil. We drain and refill engine oil regularly during oil changes, so engine oil flushes are few and far between, if they are necessary at all. If you change your oil on schedule, you shouldn't run into problems with sludge and particle buildup. But if you don't keep up with oil changes, you may need an engine oil flush. If your PCT or your owner's manual recommends one, follow their lead.

Power Steering Fluid. Power steering fluid is not maintained often, so flush the system per your owner's manual or the recommendation of your PCT.

Coolant. Depending on your driving habits, coolant should be flushed between 60,000 to 100,000 miles. Follow your owner's manual or get a recommendation from your PCT to figure out which is right for you. Once your car has been driven over 100,000 miles, you may want to consider a drain and refill every year.

Brake Fluid. Drain and refill only per your owner's manual or a recommendation from your PCT.

Windshield Washer Fluid. Drain and refill as necessary.

The Hardware

Checking and refilling fluids under the hood is the primary DIY zone, but it's still worth familiarizing yourself with the rest of the terrain. Being able to identify a part on your car may help you diagnose and explain an issue to your PCT—or give you a better grasp of things when your PCT diagnoses the issue for you.

Spark Plugs. Your spark plugs and the assorted electrical components connected to them create the spark that sets off the explosion or combustion of gasoline. The spark plug's "plug" sits inside the engine, while its wires and other components sit on top of the engine block. Spark plugs wear down with use, so PCTs regularly replace them during tune-ups, replacing the spark plug wires, the engine air filter, the PCV valve (if applicable), and the fuel filter (if applicable) at the same time.

Belts and Pulleys. One or more rubber belts sit to the right of or in front of the engine, spun by pulleys as they feed the engine's energy to several parts of the car. There's the timing belt inside the engine, and the serpentine belt outside the engine. The belts and/or pulleys will often make high-pitched whining noises when they need to be replaced. Using a flashlight if the belts are difficult to see, you can eyeball them for cracks and indications of wear.

Battery. You're going to want to locate the battery, and fortunately this part is pretty easy to identify. It may be covered by a red plastic cap or have red wires emerging from its positive side and will have two metal posts sticking out of its top. We often think of the battery as living under the hood, but in fact many cars on the road store their batteries under the backseat, with the terminals or post under the hood. You'll be touching your battery only to brush off corrosion from its posts or in the event that you need to jump-start your car, which we'll be learning to do on page 283. The terminals should be labeled positive or power, and negative or ground. Check your owner's manual if you open your hood and can't find your battery or terminals.

Alternator. Attached to the engine by the serpentine belt and pulley and located either to the right of or in front of the engine, the alternator provides the electricity that keeps the car's electrical components running, kind of like the electric company. Without the alternator, your battery would die in fifteen minutes or less. Despite being such a useful part, the alternator doesn't require maintenance, so you won't be getting up close and personal with yours.

Starter. The starter motor is the mini-motor that turns on the engine by spinning the crankshaft. Like alternators, starters don't require maintenance.

Fuse Box. Located next to the battery, the fuse box contains all ratings of fuses and relays. Fuses are easy to remove and replace if you know which one has been blown.

DIY #2: Check and Add Windshield Washer Fluid

Windshield washer fluid isn't something you probably think much about until a big fat bug decides to end its life on your windshield or a bird uses your car for target practice. But if your reservoir is running on empty, your windshield wipers will actually make things worse by spreading the bug juice or bird poop across the windshield. Gross.

Refilling your own washer fluid is the easiest, hardest-to-screw-up DIY, so no excuses on this front.

Tools
Windshield washer fluid
Funnel
Gloves (optional)

1. Locate the washer fluid reservoir under the hood of your car.

2. The reservoir may have full and low markings, or a rubber dipstick or hose attached to the cap. If the fluid is low or the rubber hose is dry, you need to add fluid.

3. Remove the cap from the reservoir and place the funnel over the opening. Add fluid to the full level. Remove the funnel and put the cap back on.

Now you can attack that bug juice with a little more ammo!

As a general rule of thumb, check your washer fluid every year. Your PCT should keep an eye on it as well.

Part ii

EVERYTHING YOU NEED TO KNOW ABOUT HOW CARS WORK

Anatomy of a Modern Car

The vehicle that gets you to work or to school or to the store every day is a complex machine containing more than ten thousand separate parts. And we're going to go through each and every single one. Just kidding! That would be crazy *and* boring. We're actually going to look at the five major components that allow your car to run. Nothing too technical or complex.

Cars don't have to be scary. They're actually pretty cool, sexy, and powerful when you get to know them. And when we build up a bit of knowledge about our cars, we can let go of the anxiety and shame that come from being in the dark.

The Powertrain

The powertrain system, also known as the drivetrain and consisting of the engine, the transmission, the driveshaft, the differentials, and the drive wheels, includes the main components that generate and distribute your vehicle's power. Despite the importance of its parts, the only time you actually hear the word *powertrain* is when you're buying a car and choosing between a powertrain warranty and a bumper-to-bumper warranty (see page 265.) So congratulations on already being one step ahead of the average car buyer!

The Engine and the Emissions System

Located front and center under your hood, the engine is a mechanical workhorse designed to replace the work of animals or humans. And just as animals and people need food for energy before they can work, engines need food for the important work they do. This food is fuel or gas, and the engine takes that fuel and sets it on fire in a series of mini-explosions. These mini-explosions inside the engine are what make your car go.

The single most important part of a car, the engine requires frequent, *in*expensive maintenance—but any repairs will be expensive.

Emissions, a corollary system, has to do with controlling the vapors and exhaust created by the engine's mini-explosions.

The Transmission

The transmission system moves (or transmits) power from the engine to the wheels of the car. Transmissions can be either automatic (the car shifts into higher or lower gear depending on how much power you're asking of it at any given moment) or manual (the driver uses her clutch and gearshift like a boss to tell the car when it's time to kick it up or down a notch). Like the engine, a trans is very expensive to replace and very inexpensive to maintain, but unlike the engine, it doesn't require frequent maintenance.

The Chassis

A weird word with a silent *s* at the end, the chassis (pronounced "chassie") supports the weight of the engine, the transmission, and the car's occupants, and also allows the car to move in a straight line, turn, and stop. The chassis is made up of four components:

Body/Frame. The body or frame supports the weight of the car, just like the foundation of a house. Made of steel, it's a low-maintenance part that requires attention if it has rusted or corroded over time or if it has been damaged by a collision.

Suspension. Your car's suspension system ensures a nice smooth ride, keeping all the tires on the road when you go over bumps, rocks, or potholes. You can't see your suspension system, but you'll feel and hear suspension problems. Suspension parts are all underneath the car, which means they can be accessed only when the car is off the ground, on a lift or jack stands.

Brakes. We all know what brakes do—slow down the rotation of your wheels, in turn slowing down the car. Brakes come in two types, disc and drum, and they give drivers audible information about their condition. Listen to your brakes.

Steering, Wheels, and Tires. Your car has six wheels. Nope, not a typo. Count 'em—two front, two rear, the steering wheel (the command center for all the other wheels in the car), and the spare. Wheels work in tandem with your tires to stop, accelerate, and turn your car. Like the heels on a favorite pair of shoes, the tires of your car require frequent but easy upkeep. And yes, on page 197 you'll be learning how to change one.

The Electrical System and the Computers in Your Car

A modern car requires a ton of electricity to run, and auto manufacturers add new electrical features every year. You've got your obvious electrical components—headlights, GPS, the thing that used to be called a radio, dashboard lights, and any automated seating, door closure, or window controls. And your not-so-obvious electrical components—the battery, starter, and alternator, which happen to be much more central to the process of actually running a car.

The word *electrical* doesn't have the same meaning as it did in the old days. Now it includes the scores of small computers (also sometimes known as control modules), sensors, and switches that regulate emissions, run onboard diagnostics, control vehicle operations, deploy the air bags, and much more. Any of these components can be affected by an electrical malfunction. Electrical and electronic issues can cause an engine to run rough, safety features to malfunction, a passenger window to get stuck, or a car to fail to start. They can be tough to figure out and may involve lots of diagnosing and problem solving.

Heating and Air-Conditioning

Many drivers mistakenly assume that their heat and AC come from a single unified system. In fact, only the air delivery portion is shared. The AC runs off Freon, a chemical refrigerant, and is driven by a compressor that requires the engine to burn a bit of additional gas to keep you cozy; the heater runs off redirected engine heat and hot coolant.

There are hundreds of other parts connecting the dots, but these major systems are all you really need to run a car. We'll learn more about each system in more detail in the coming chapters.

The "Three E's": Engines, Exhaust, Emissions

Engines are powerful, sophisticated—and expensive to repair or replace. Which is why consistent engine maintenance is essential, for the health of both your car and your wallet.

Remember those miniature explosions? The engine is where it all goes down. Also known as the motor, the engine is not one thing but a mass of metal shafts, cylinders, rods, pistons, and gears that spin, rotate, or slide. Those actions generate the power that feeds the transmission and wheels, the power steering pump, the AC, and the components that provide electricity to the car. But what gives the internal combustion engines used in standard vehicles their juice? Gasoline, aka fuel. That's not all there is to it, of course.

The First E Is for Engine: The Three Stages of Combustion

In a little bit more detail, let's talk about how the engine does its job, guzzling all that tasty gasoline and turning it into motion. You need three things in order for the engine to run: air, fuel, and spark (fire). These three elements are involved in a four-part digestive process that happens continuously until you turn the car off.

I call it the Eat, Burn, Belch cycle.

Eat. As soon as you turn the key in the ignition and start the car, fuel is pumped from your fuel tank, in the rear of the vehicle, into the hungry engine. Inside the engine, fuel is "injected" with air pulled in from the outside of the car, and the air-fuel mixture is compressed to an extremely high temperature and pressure.

Burn. Within the engine's belly, the compressed air-and-fuel mixture is set on fire by spark plugs. Lighting the hot, pressurized gas creates an explosion, or combustion, inside the cylinders. A single spark plug can fire four hundred times per minute, so you get just as many mini-explosions in that tiny amount of time. Science, amiright?

Belch. After the air-and-fuel mixture is set on fire, the engine blows out the exhaust (the remnants of combustion) through a long pipe.

Repeat. The cycle constantly repeats itself as your car runs. Eat, Burn, Belch, repeat!

Fuel: You Are What You Eat

Without fuel, the engine can't function. But how does gas get from the fuel tank into the engine, and what happens once it's there? The following components are involved.

Fuel Pump. Propelled by an electric motor and sitting inside the gas tank, the fuel pump moves raw fuel or gas from the back of the car to the engine. The fuel pump will fail from use over time, or from the strain of pumping from a tank that's too low on gas.

Fuel Injectors. The fuel injectors spray raw fuel from the gas tank into the engine.

Fuel Pressure Regulator. The fuel pressure regulator monitors fuel output. A regulator failure can cause engine flooding and, in the worst-case scenario, fire.

Fuel Filter. The fuel filter strains out dirt, particles, and foreign objects from raw fuel before they can enter the engine.

Fuel Lines and Hoses. These rigid metal tubes and flexible rubber hoses supply raw fuel from the gas tank to the engine. Hoses will fail from use over time, and hose leaks may prevent a car from starting.

Gas Tank. The gas tank holds raw gasoline.

Gas Cap. The gas cap seals off the fuel system to prevent gas vapors from escaping and polluting the environment. Its rubber gasket will fail from use over time, but you can purchase a replacement for less than thirty dollars.

Your Engine's Nutritional Ratio

As the Eat, Burn, Belch cycle demonstrates, air, fuel, and spark are crucial for the engine to run. The air and fuel taken in by the mouth of your engine must also be calibrated to a certain ratio for all of the tiny explosions to take place. That golden ratio is approximately 14.7 to 1, air to fuel— meaning you need 14.7 times more air than gasoline to run an engine. You can't start a campfire without good airflow, and the same is true of internal combustion.

Spark: The Ignition System

The ignition system's most important job is sending electricity from the car's battery to the spark plugs inside each engine cylinder. The system is composed of the following components:

Spark Plugs. Using a huge electric jolt, of 40,000 volts, spark plugs set off your engine's mini-explosions. Small devices that create bolts of lightning, the spark plugs light sparks that burn the compressed air-fuel mixture inside the engine's cylinders. Spark plugs vary in price, but the more expensive plugs will last longer. They generally need replacing during "tune-ups" at 80,000 to 100,000 miles (see box, page 58), or per your owner's manual.

Ignition Coil (if applicable). The ignition coil sends electricity to the spark plugs.

Distributor Cap and Rotor (if applicable). The distributor cap and rotor distribute electricity to each spark plug.

Spark Plug Wires (if applicable). These wires help deliver electricity to the spark plugs from the cap and rotor.

Air: Does Your Engine Have Boogies?

I used to hate it when mechanics told me I needed to plunk down an extra thirty bucks to replace my engine air filter after I'd finally dragged myself in for an oil change. They'd say something about engine performance or gas mileage and I'd usually tune them out. This was a mistake. Engine air filters aren't upsells. Remember how those mini-explosions inside the engine can't happen without a ratio of fourteen parts air to one part fuel? The air in that mixture is sucked into the engine straight from the outside world. It's the same air we breathe, and it's filled with dust and dirt and contaminants.

If you don't change your engine air filter per your owner's man-

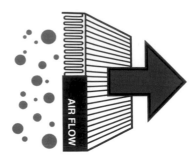

The air filter prevents dust and dirt from entering the engine.

ual, your engine will have a hard time breathing, just like you would with a congested nose. And yes, as those mechanics told me, your engine performance will drop. Go too long, and you might even cause that check-engine light to come on. Ugh!

The air intake system has two other significant parts: a throttle body and a mass airflow sensor. The **throttle body** controls the amount of air flowing into the engine. The **mass airflow sensor** measures the air being delivered to the engine, balancing things out by communicating with the PCM and the fuel injector to spray in additional gas. What you're actually doing when you press on the "gas" pedal is opening up the throttle body to send more air into the engine; to maintain the correct air-to-gas ratio, the mass airflow sensor kicks in and talks to the PCM. Throttle body replacements can be tricky, and the part itself is expensive—repairs can run $500 or more.

Signs of a Spark, Fuel, or Air System Issue

PROBLEM: Your car turns on, but the engine won't turn over.

CAUSE: Fuel pump, fuel pressure regulator, ignition/spark system, or air delivery issues. Tow the car to your PCT for diagnosis.

PROBLEM: Your engine misfires or runs poorly.

CAUSE: Your spark plugs are worn down and you likely need a tune-up.

PROBLEM: You lose power when you try to accelerate.

CAUSE: Likely an air delivery issue. The throttle body or mass airflow sensor may need replacing.

PROBLEM: You smell gas while you're driving.

CAUSE: Possible fuel and/or oil leak. Your check-engine light may illuminate. Take your car to your PCT as soon as possible. Driving around with a fuel leak can be very dangerous.

PROBLEM: The check-engine light is illuminated on the dashboard.

CAUSE: Your engine is not burning fuel efficiently.

Know Your Engine

The engine parts that allow the Eat, Burn, Belch cycle to eat up all that fuel and air include shafts, rods, belts, pulleys, and gears— internal parts that spin, rotate, or slide, rubbing up against each other as they work. All this movement causes wear and tear, and in this section, we are going to talk about how these parts work.

The Crankshaft

The crankshaft has the engine's most important job: its spinning motion powers all of the car's major systems. Inside the engine, the crankshaft is responsible for:

Located inside the engine and connected to many parts inside and outside the engine by rods, belts, pulleys, and gears, the crankshaft causes internal and external parts to rotate along with it.

- Opening the engine, so it can eat up air and fuel

- Closing the engine after it lets out exhaust or belches

- Burning the air and fuel inside the engine

Outside the engine, the crankshaft:

- Powers the transmission and wheels

- Powers the AC compressor

- Powers the power steering pump

- Powers the water pump, which pumps coolant through the engine

- Powers the air pump, which pumps air into the exhaust

- Powers the alternator, which provides *all* electricity to the car while it is running

Located along the bottom of the engine, the crankshaft is responsible for a tremendous amount of work, and it lasts for hundreds of thousands of miles. That's a good thing. Engines are so complex, with so much riding on them, that we need them to be workhorses that will go the distance for the length of our vehicular relationships.

Belts

Two rubber belts connect the crankshaft to internal and external parts of the engine.

The first, near the crankshaft, is an internal belt called a **timing belt**. When the crankshaft spins, the timing belt spins and activates the water pump. The engine is eating, burning, and belching; if the timing belt doesn't drive the water pump, the **serpentine belt** does. Most cars have timing belts, but a few have timing chains, which look like thick bicycle chains and don't need to be replaced.

When the timing belt spins, an idler pulley also transfers power to the serpentine belt, a rubber belt outside the engine that is sometimes called a drive belt. (You located it under the hood on

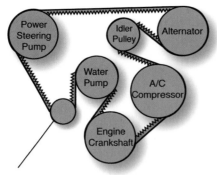

The pulleys that transfer the engine's power are connected through a continuous belt (see serpentine belt); the belt assembly is mounted to the outside of your engine.

Belt Tensioner

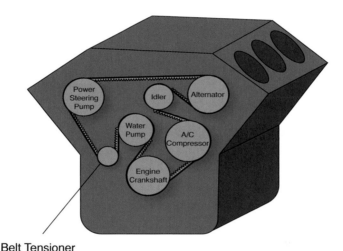

Belt Tensioner

page 73.) The serpentine belt connects the engine crankshaft to all of the systems mentioned before—the pulleys that power the alternator, power steering, AC compressor, and more.

Cylinders

V8 isn't just a mixer for your favorite brunchtime beverage.

It's also where the engine Eats, sucking air and fuel into separate compartments called cylinders before moving on to the Burn cycle.

Combustion engines come in several types, but the most common are inline-four, V-6, and V-8. The numbers reference the quantity of cylinders inside the engine. An inline-four engine has four cylinders, a V-6 has six cylinders, and so on. The more cylinders in your engine, the more fuel you will need—and the faster and more powerful your car will be. Trucks, SUVs, and race cars tend to have V-8 engines, which give them the power to accelerate quickly or to haul or tow heavy objects.

What does the letter *V* have to do with it? That's the shape the cylinders make as they sit inside the engine. There are also inline-five, inline-six, V-10, and V-12 engines, but they are less common and usually seen in European models, sports cars, Jeeps, and luxury vehicles.

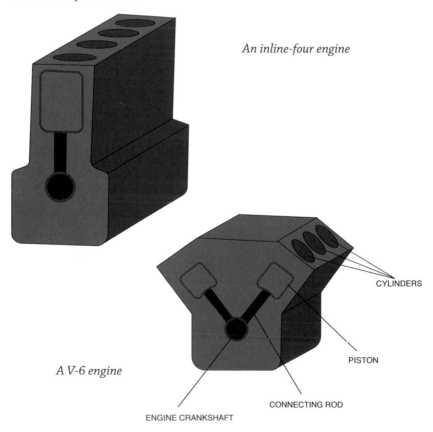

An inline-four engine

CYLINDERS

A V-6 engine

PISTON

CONNECTING ROD

ENGINE CRANKSHAFT

Do You Need Horsepower?

You've definitely heard the term, and you've probably wondered what it means. Essentially, horsepower is the amount of power the car can produce. And only people who buy cars for speed and power need to worry about it.

Horsepower also has to do with the amount of power the engine can generate by playing with the Burn portion of the Eat, Burn, Belch cycle. Engines that set fuel on fire at higher temperatures also efficiently compress fuel and air for added power. These engines take premium gas and other premium fluids designed to burn at higher temperatures, and they're outfitted with spark plugs that spark at higher temperatures. The greater your engine's power, the greater the torque (the power that is transferred to the wheels), the faster the car accelerates and drives.

The Tachometer and Crankshaft

Wouldn't it be cool if the tachometer were an app telling us the location of the nearest taco place? Instead it's the dashboard instrument that measures how fast the crankshaft inside the engine is spinning.

When you're idling and only a tiny bit of gas is being fed into the engine, the tachometer runs around a 1. On a highway, it hovers around 2.5 or 3, and on a hill, the dial can point to 4 or 5. Sound slow? Those numbers actually stand for thousands of rpm (revolutions per minute). At highway speeds, your crankshaft is spinning 2,500 to 3,000 times per minute.

Whoa! That crankshaft is one fast piece of machinery. The faster it rotates, the faster the Eat, Burn, Belch cycle spins, and the more lubrication is required. Getting the needle to 7 or 8 is what we call *redlining*, when the crankshaft is moving so fast that the whole engine is becoming unstable. In the redline zone, the engine's internal parts are spinning way too fast, and the engine may become unstable and blow up.

To tell you the truth, most drivers don't pay much attention to the tachometer, and that's okay. But if you're concerned about saving money on gas, you'll want the tachometer hovering around 2 as often as possible. And if you notice the tachometer wildly jumping up and down, especially during acceleration, there may be a problem with the amount of air or fuel being delivered to your engine.

INTERNAL AND EXTERNAL ENGINE PARTS
MAINTENANCE AND REPAIRS

PART	ISSUE	FIX	TIMING	COST
Timing Belt	Made of rubber, timing belts don't last forever	A timing belt's location inside the engine makes it difficult to access, so replacing one is a very expensive repair. Note: If your car has a timing *chain*, no maintenance is needed	PCTs cannot routinely check to see if a timing belt is going bad, so we recommend replacing yours around 100,000 miles. Ignore this important maintenance task and the timing belt can fail on the road, causing far more expensive damage	Look to spend at least $650 to replace
Drive/ Serpentine Belt and Pulleys	The drive or serpentine belt and pulleys that attach the alternator, power steering pump, and other parts of the engine crankshaft will fail from use over time. Because the belts are made of rubber for flexibility, they will wear down. The pulleys will seize up and stop spinning	Look for cracks in the belt, perpendicular to the ribs. The car may make a high-pitched or chirping noise when you first turn it on, while it is in drive, or during acceleration. When you hear this, it's time to replace the belt and one or more pulleys	Belts reach the end of their life span at around 60,000–120,000 miles, depending on the vehicle model	Normally less than $150
Gaskets and Seals	Gaskets and seals prevent oil and coolant from leaking inside and outside the engine. They will fail and break down from use over time, causing fuel leaks	Replace gasket or seal	Shouldn't fail before 60,000– 80,000 miles	$500+. Could go over $1,500 if labor is intensive

ENGINE LUBRICATION SYSTEM
MAINTENANCE AND REPAIRS

PART	ISSUE	FIX	TIMING	COST
Engine Oil and Oil Filter	All internal parts must be lubricated for optimal functioning	Your PCT will drain the old oil, replace the oil filter, and put in fresh oil	See your owner's manual	$40–$95, depending on the oil
Oil Pump	Wears over time. If the oil pump fails, pressurized oil won't be pumped through the system	Replace	Your dashboard oilcan light will alert you to a failure	$750+
Oil Pan and Gasket	The oil pan gasket can fail, causing oil to leak from the oil pan. The oil pan itself can fail from corrosion and will need to be replaced	Replace	Variable	$750+

No Lube, No Action: Your Engine's Lubrication System

The engine's Eat, Burn, Belch cycle happens at incredibly high speeds, generating a huge amount of heat and friction. It's not just the explosions that make things so hot, it's also the demonically fast spinning of the internal parts and the firing of the spark plugs. Recall how fast the crankshaft is spinning: three thousand times per minute when you are driving. All that motion and friction create tons of heat. Enter oil, your engine's lifeline, the essential fluid that lubricates the engine to protect it from friction. Engine oil keeps things working in harmony by creating a slippery coat that allows internal parts to move with ease. Without it, your engine is toast. So get to know your under-the-hood lubrication system, which contains the following components.

Engine Oil. Fluid that lubricates moving and sliding internal engine parts (also known as motor oil). Because engines contain many moving and sliding parts, their inner workings must be lubricated to reduce friction and wear. It is essential to keep oil running through your engine at all times. See page 97 for information on what type of oil to feed yours.

Oil Pump. A pump turned by the engine crankshaft to move pressurized oil through an oil filter and to the engine.

Oil Pan and Gasket. Where the oil is stored. Most cars hold 5 liters, but larger cars hold more. The oil pan attaches to the bottom of the engine and is sealed with a rubber gasket to prevent leaks.

Oil Filter. Strains dirt and foreign objects from oil before they reach the engine.

TIP: *Have you ever noticed that when you're overdue for an oil change, your engine runs a little rough? And that as soon as you get an oil change, the engine feels like it is purring? The next time you are due for an oil change, don't procrastinate.*

Conventional Oil, Synthetic Oil, or Synthetic Blend?

Pre–auto tech Patrice didn't take too kindly to being asked what type of oil she wanted in her car. "Huh? Shouldn't *you* know that?" I'd ask the tech at the quick-lube facility in a slightly irritated tone. He'd try to explain the difference between synthetic and conventional, but I'd cut the conversation short when I found out synthetic was going to be more than twice the price. "Nah, I'm good. I'll just take the thirty-five-dollar oil change, please." No one was going to upsell me!

But synthetic oil is not an upsell. Depending on your car, it may be helpful or even necessary.

Do you drive a luxury car? If the answer is no, your car most likely uses regular oil. **Conventional oil** or **regular oil** is what most cars (think Hondas, Fords) take today. You can get an oil change with regular oil for less than forty dollars almost anywhere in the United States.

Luxury cars (think Lexus, Mercedes, BMW, Audi) take **synthetic oil,** sometimes called **full synthetic.** Created by oil engineers who used additives to manufacture an oil far superior in quality, synthetic oil lasts longer, performs better, and is cleaner than conventional or regular oil. It is also two to three times the price. Expect to spend at least sixty-five and as much as ninety-five dollars on a synthetic oil change.

Synthetic blend, aka **high-mileage oil,** is a combination of conventional and synthetic oils. Once your car has accumulated a large amount of mileage (100,000 miles or more), you may want to consider using this blend to get some of synthetic's superior performance at a lower cost. Most new cars require synthetic blends. Expect to spend forty-five to sixty-five dollars on a synthetic blend oil change.

If conventional oil is a regular manicure, synthetic is a fancy gel situation. If you have a luxury car, you *must* use synthetic oil, so no regular manis for you. For everyone else, the choice of regular or synthetic (high-mileage) oil just depends on whether you want to spend a little bit of extra cash for a better product. Gel manicures are going to be higher quality and last longer, but a standard car doesn't really need synthetic or a blend/high-mileage oil, just like nobody really needs a gel manicure.

Switching between synthetic and conventional oil isn't a cardinal sin. However, mixing the two types of oil is a no-no. If you need to add oil to the engine but aren't draining out the existing oil, stick with the same grade you were using before.

Oil Type

What do the alphanumerical combinations 10W-30 and 5W-20 mean to you? These letters and numbers specify different types of engine oil, which vary in viscosity and thickness. To find out the oil type your car requires, check the oil filler cap on your engine or refer to your owner's manual. You can also search online or go to a parts store and give them your car's year, make, and model. P.S. Some people may call it weight, but the *W* stands for *winter,* meaning that the oil is okay to use in harsh cold-weather conditions, like negative temperatures.

Oil Changes vs. Refills

An oil *refill* is something any ♪#shecanic can accomplish if her oil is low, requiring nothing more than a bottle of engine oil and a funnel. An oil *change* is something a mechanic performs when the oil has reached the end of its life (normally 5,000–10,000 miles). Oil changes involve parts and a whole bunch of tools—a wrench that fits the oil pan bolt, an oil filter wrench, a jack for the car, two jack stands to lift the car, a bucket to put the used oil in—not to mention a means of safely and legally disposing of the used oil. The parts alone will add up to the cost of getting the job done at your local repair shop, so changing your own oil doesn't come out as a win unless you regularly perform other maintenance and repairs on your car.

Signs of a Lubrication System Issue

Any issues involving engine oil need to be addressed ASAP, before they cause expensive damage to your engine. Look out for the following signs of a problem.

> **PROBLEM:** Oil leak
>
> **CAUSE:** Oil leaks often occur around the engine's seals and gaskets. You'll be able to see an oil leak, either under the hood or underneath the car. Have a mechanic check it out ASAP to determine the extent of the leak and how much it will cost to repair.
>
> **PROBLEM:** Lack of oil or oil pump failure
>
> **CAUSE:** This is caused by the engine overheating.
>
> **PROBLEM:** Engine noises
>
> **CAUSE:** Lack of oil. A quick tapping in the engine likely means there is no oil.

TIP: *Listen up,* ♪#shecanic. *When it comes to your engine, noise will often be your indication of an internal issue. Take your car in to your PCT if you hear any clicking, clacking, knocking, rattling, clattering, whining, or clunking noises coming from under the hood.*

Hot Stuff: Your Engine's Cooling System

A mixture of antifreeze and water, coolant is pumped through the engine to maintain an optimal internal temperature of approximately 220 degrees Fahrenheit—still hotter than any desert on earth. Internal combustion is no joke. Temperatures inside the engine's cylinders reach up to 4,500 degrees Fahrenheit, and exhaust

COOLANT SYSTEM: MAINTENANCE AND REPAIRS

PART	ISSUE	FIX	TIMING	COST
Coolant	Coolant picks up dirt and particles over the years. These cause clogs within the system, especially in the heater core, making the car likely to overheat	A fluid flush. There is no filter for coolant, so flushes are extremely important. If a clog can't be flushed out, the clogged section will need to be replaced	Coolant may be discolored. Rule of thumb is three to five years—check your maintenance schedule. If the car has more than 100,000 miles, consider a drain and refill every year	$100 or less
Water Pump	The water pump can fail from wear over time, commonly leaking coolant at its connection point to the engine	If the pump is driven by the timing belt, replace both parts when either one fails	The engine will overheat	$750+
Thermostat	The valve that controls coolant flow can leak or stick open or closed. The needle on your dashboard temperature gauge will read at C or H rather than staying in the middle	Replace	The engine will overheat or won't warm up to its optimal temperature	Varies greatly depending on the car, but most can be done for under $150
Radiator	The radiator will fail from use over time, leaking coolant and causing the car to overheat if neglected	Replace	Variable, after 80,000–100,000 miles	Look to spend at least $300

PART	ISSUE	FIX	TIMING	COST
Coolant Hoses	Fail from use over time. Sometimes a hot oil or coolant leak will drip onto the rubber hoses, causing them to soften and split. Coolant can leak through a softened rubber hose	Replace	The car will overheat	$100 or less
Fan	Fails from use over time. When it does, the car will likely overheat as you idle at a light or drive at low speeds	Replace	The car will overheat	$500+

gas temperatures hover around 1,500 degrees. Working at such high heat would weaken internal parts and cause the engine to fail, so it must be cooled to a relatively breezy 220 degrees in order to continue to function. That job falls to the liquid coolant that is pumped through the engine. But a fluid can't circulate on its lonesome, so here's a list of the parts that help monitor the engine's temperature and maintain it within a safe range.

Coolant. The fluid that maintains optimal engine temperature and prevents corrosion. Coolant mainly comes in two types, 70/30 (70 percent antifreeze to 30 percent water) and 50/50 (equal parts antifreeze and water).

Coolant Reservoir. The bottle in which excess coolant is stored.

Water Pump. The component that pushes coolant through the thermostat, engine, and radiator. (Cars initially used water as coolant, and the name stuck around.)

Thermostat. The valve or faucet that controls coolant and engine temperature by (1) opening when the engine gets too hot, allowing coolant to flow from the engine to the radiator to cool down, and (2) closing when the engine is too cold, restricting the flow of coolant to the radiator, hence warming up the engine.

Radiator. The part where coolant flows to cool down after it passes through the super-hot engine. When the coolant gets too hot, it can boil or evaporate as steam.

Fan. The cooling mechanism, which sits in front of the radiator and condenser, blowing air past the radiator to bring down the coolant's temperature. It also blows air past the condenser used by the AC and heating (see page 223).

Coolant Hoses. The rubber tubes connecting the radiator to the engine, through which hot pressurized coolant flows.

A loop of coolant is continuously pumping through your cooling system as your car runs—wrapping around the engine, flowing through the radiator, and then making its way back to the engine. As the coolant touches the surface of the engine, it picks up heat via heat transfer, then moves to the radiator to release that heat before being sent right back to the engine. This cycle keeps the engine running at optimal temperature.

Coolant and Your Dashboard

How do you know your coolant is doing its job? Check out the C to H (cold to hot) temperature gauge on your dashboard. (European vehicles tend to use numbers that designate coolant temperature in Celsius.) When you start your car, the needle will be on C. Your engine is cold, the coolant is cold, and the thermostat is closed. Depending on external temperatures and how long the car has been turned off, it takes one to ten minutes for the needle to hit the middle of the gauge—the happy spot. Like Goldilocks's porridge, coolant temperature needs to be "just right" to keep your engine content.

Too cold? If the needle doesn't reach the middle of the gauge after ten minutes of driving, there is too much coolant circulating to the engine. Your thermostat is most likely stuck open, continuously sending coolant to the radiator.

Just right? The needle reaches the middle of the temperature gauge a few minutes after you start the car and stays there. The engine and coolant are running at optimal temperature. The needle shouldn't move from the middle position until you turn the car off again.

Too hot? If the needle starts to creep up past the middle of the gauge, the engine is overheating. A message or coolant light may come up on the dash, and you might see smoke rising from under the hood. The engine is reaching unsafe temperatures. Coolant isn't circulating through the radiator, and it will start to boil off or evaporate as its temperature increases, leaving no coolant in the system. Three things could be going on: The thermostat is stuck closed, there's a block somewhere preventing coolant from circulating, or you've sprung a coolant leak somewhere. If you continue to drive, you are in danger of damaging your engine. (Remember what happened to my beloved poop car?) Shut off your vehicle as soon as it is safe to do so, and see page 277 for more on what to do next.

The Second E Is for Exhaust: Smelly Burps and Droopy Tailpipes

Burping at the dinner table may be rude, but the belch of combusted air coming from the tailpipe is essential to the proper functioning of your car. Though that belch feeds the smog layer in traffic-heavy cities like L.A., in newer cars it's become a lot less polluting.

In both traditional and hybrid cars, the exhaust system is basically a line of pipe running under the car, but it does have a few distinct components. The only maintenance these items require is an easy-breezy car wash to keep snow, salt, and sand from corroding metal parts.

Exhaust Pipe. The long metal pipe through which extremely hot exhaust gas is blown out of the engine.

Flex Pipe. A section of the exhaust pipe that is a flexible hose, allowing the hot pipe to move or breathe a little. The exhaust gas coming out the tailpipe is hot and moving fast, so the pipe needs to be flexible and stretchy to accommodate for movement and drastic changes in temperature.

Muffler and Tailpipe. The muffler dampens the loud sound exhaust makes as it travels through the exhaust pipe. The end of the muffler is the tailpipe, the exit point for the engine's exhaust gas and the part pranksters like to plug with potatoes.

Gaskets. Used to seal metal pipe connections.

Hangers. Metal brackets that hold the exhaust pipe on to the car. You'll notice these are missing when your car's tailpipe drags on the ground.

I'll discuss exhaust system maintenance and repairs along with the emissions system after the next section.

The Third E Is for Emissions: Monitoring Your Junk

Every bit of the air-and-fuel mixture that goes into your engine eventually comes out, but with an essential chemical difference due to the fact that it has been burned. And this mixture that comes out is not so nice to our environment. That's why cars are equipped with emissions systems designed to monitor and control the fuel delivery system's performance. Your emissions system ensures that you're not using too much gas or sending too much junk out your tailpipe and excessively polluting our air, water, and land. If there's a problem with your emissions system, your dashboard will let you know by turning on the check-engine light.

Loaded up with controls, computers, valves, switches, and sensors, the emissions system contains the following components:

Catalytic Converter (CC). Fuel isn't uniformly burned off during the engine's mini-explosions; it leaves behind a mixture of raw fuel (not environmentally friendly) and burned exhaust gas (more environmentally friendly). We don't want raw, unburned fuel or other pollutants in the air we breathe, so the catalytic converter saves the day by transforming any unburned or raw fuel to gas before it gets blown out through the tailpipe.

Air Pump. The air pump injects fresh air into the exhaust system to help reduce pollutants and lessen the load on the catalytic converter.

Positive Crankcase Ventilation (PCV) Valve. Small amounts of combustion gases hang around past the Eat, Burn, Belch cycle. Instead of exiting via the exhaust pipe, they "blow by" the internal engine parts instead. The PCV valve collects those gases and circulates them back into the air-fuel intake system so they don't wind up polluting the environment.

Exhaust Gas Recirculation (EGR) Valve. The EGR valve helps the engine burn fuel more efficiently by rerouting a small amount of exhaust gas back into the engine.

Oxygen or O_2 Sensor. The oxygen sensor measures the amount of oxygen in the exhaust stream to ensure optimal burn. If there's too much air in the ratio (mechanics call this being too lean in fuel), the system will inject additional fuel into the engine. If there is too little oxygen (mechanics call this being too rich in fuel), the system will inject less fuel into the engine.

Evaporative Control System. The evaporative control system collects raw (unburned) fuel vapors from the gas tank and pumps them to the engine to be burned. Beware of damaging your evaporative charcoal canister by topping off the gas at the pump.

Passing Inspections in Your State

Do you need to get your car regularly inspected to pass safety and emissions requirements? Safety and smog checks are regulated by individual states, so the answer depends on where you live. California has the strictest standards, but in many states, no inspections are required. In Maine, they're required annually, while in Delaware, they apply only to cars five years and older. In some states, the testing is done directly by the motor vehicle department, while in others, any repair shop outfitted with state-approved equipment and certified techs can perform emissions testing. The regulations are all over the place, so check your state's official guidelines online to find out what you need to do. (You may also receive a notification from the state when it's time to renew your registration.)

Be aware that anywhere you test, an illuminated check-engine light will cause you to fail inspection. Your PCT will have to determine the problem's root cause in order for your car to pass.

Oil Leaks

As you start racking up miles on your car, oil leaks will begin to happen around the seals and gaskets of the engine and oil pan. These components are designed to prevent oil from leaking at joints where parts come together, but they do wear out. Fixing an oil leak can get very expensive, so some car owners choose to monitor the leak and add oil to the engine as needed to compensate, a technique that isn't recommended, particularly when it comes to larger leaks. If you find yourself needing to add oil to your engine once a week, it's in your best interest to repair the leak.

Your mechanic will check for leaks every time you take your car in for service, but signs of a leak include oil dripping under the car or on parts under the hood. Additives that claim to slow down or stop oil leaks do not really work, so don't bother with them.

EXHAUST AND EMISSIONS SYSTEMS
MAINTENANCE AND REPAIRS

PART	ISSUE	FIX	TIMING	COST
Metal Exhaust Pipes or Metal Flexible Exhaust Hoses	Corrosion from exhaust gases will cause these steel pieces to rust over time, leading to leaks. In areas prone to winter weather, the salt and sand used to melt ice and snow can corrode these metal parts	Protect your exhaust piping from salt corrosion with an annual undercarriage wash once winter turns to spring. Exhaust pipes can sometimes be repaired by welding, but flex pipes must be replaced	The check-engine light may illuminate, and/or you may hear embarrassingly loud rumbles and noises when you drive and accelerate	Varies depending on the location of the leak and whether the pipe can be repaired or needs to be replaced. Normally less than $500
Muffler	Mufflers corrode and acquire holes. You'll hear a car in need of a new muffler from blocks away—it's loud!	Replace	Embarrassingly loud rumbles and noises when you drive and accelerate	Average cost of less than $250
Rubber Gaskets	Over time rubber gaskets will lose their elasticity and ability to seal off pipe connections	Replace	Slight rumbles and soft noises when you drive and accelerate	Less than $150
Hangers	Hangers can corrode or get knocked out of place. Ever see an old car with its tailpipe dragging on the ground? It needs a hanger replaced!	Replace	When the tailpipe starts to drag	Less than $100

PART	ISSUE	FIX	TIMING	COST
Catalytic Converter	Catalytic converters fail from use over time, leading to an increase in pollutants escaping into the environment	Replace	Check-engine light will illuminate	Expect to pay at least $500
Air Pump	Air pumps fail from use over time, leading to an increase in pollutants escaping into the environment	Replace	Check-engine light will illuminate	Expect to pay at least $500
Oxygen Sensor, EGR, and PCV Valves	These sensors and valves fail from use over time	Replace	Check-engine light will illuminate	PCV valves cost less than $100 to replace. EGR valve replacements vary, from $150–$350. Oxygen sensor replacements vary, from $150–$500
EVAP Charcoal Canister	This canister can be damaged by topping off gas when filling the tank or from use over time	Replace	Check-engine light will illuminate	$300-$600

DIY #3:
How to Check and Add Oil

If there's one thing I want to accomplish in this book, it's convincing ♪#shecanics everywhere that engine oil is just as important to the health of your cars as gasoline. Actually, more! Oil is your car's lifeline. We think more about gas, partly because we're refilling that tank on the regular. And since most of us aren't taught to change our oil, it just becomes one of those mysterious under-the-hood things auto airheads *love* to ignore.

Your days of oil illiteracy are over. In this section, we're going to learn all about checking and refilling our own oil. Listen, I get it. Some of you are going to be pumped about tackling this. Some of you are already pros at checking and topping off your oil and don't even need these instructions. And a few of you are checking your cuticles and getting ready to skip ahead. But even if you still plan to take your car to the mechanic for this job (and most of us will), I want you to understand what's involved.

Consider this a lesson in auto care CPR. You may never need to use it, but one day it might save your life. And your very expensive engine.

How and When to Check Your Oil

Normally, you'll get things checked out every six months at your regularly scheduled maintenance appointments, and anytime your oil change monitor pipes up. But there are a few circumstances in which manually checking your oil yourself is necessary:

- Before going on a road trip longer than two hours
- Monthly once the car passes the 100,000-mile mark
- Weekly if you have a small oil leak

That may sound like a lot. But checking your oil takes only two minutes and requires no tools or props other than a rag or a paper towel and gloves. Here's how it's done:

1. Park the car on level ground and turn off the engine. Checking the oil on a hill will result in an inaccurate reading.

2. Pop your hood (remember how we learned to do that on page 64?) and locate the oil dipstick. The dipstick is a long rod that sits inside your engine and oil pan (the container that holds the engine oil). The head of the dipstick is usually a bright orange or yellow ring, making it easy to spot.

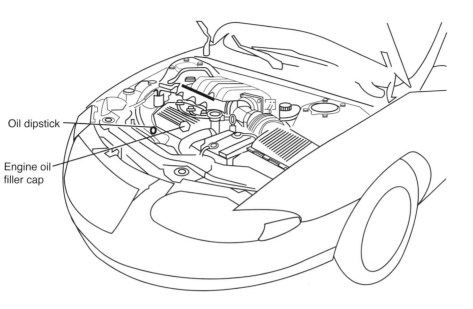

Oil dipstick

Engine oil
filler cap

The head of the oil dipstick is usually a bright orange or yellow ring.

3. Pull the dipstick all the way out, paying attention to the location of the small hole it came out of. Wipe off the dipstick with your rag or paper towel, then take a look at the indicator marks. A typical dipstick has two marks: F (Full) and L (Low); Min and Max; or two dots or lines.

4. Place the dipstick back in the hole and push it all the way down into the engine. The tip of the dipstick will reach the oil pan.

5. Pull the dipstick all the way out and read the oil level on its tip. You want the level to be between the F and L or Max and Min indicators.

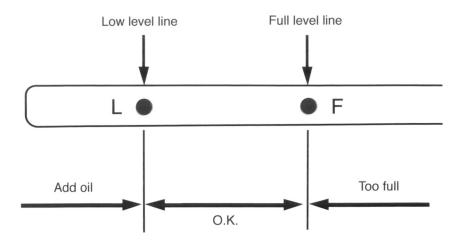

*Engines on almost all cars hold 4 to 5 quarts of oil, and, ideally,
the oil level will be full or close to full.*

An oil level at or below minimum or low needs to be dealt with ASAP. But you don't want to overfill the engine and oil pan either. Too much oil in your engine will increase pressure and could lead to your blowing an engine head gasket. If the level is too high, take your car to your PCT and have some of the oil drained off.

If there's no oil on your dipstick (mechanics call this bone dry), there is little to no oil in your engine and you are at risk of causing major damage. Either you have a leak somewhere, or you haven't changed your oil in a really, really long time. You will need to add at least 3 quarts of oil and then take your car to a mechanic to have things checked out.

If the oil level is at the Min or Low mark, your engine is probably pretty unhappy. You're likely to need an oil change (not just a refill), and you may notice your car running a little rougher. It's missing that good lube! Take your car in for an oil change as soon as possible; if you've just had an oil change, you may have a leak, so turn right around and pay another visit to your PCT.

How does the oil look? Dark brown or black oil needs to be changed. Black particles usually indicate a lack of regular oil changes and some sludge buildup in the engine. Your PCT may recommend a fluid flush to clean things up.

How to Add Oil to Your Engine

If you haven't already, it's time to head to the parts store to pick up the right type of oil for your engine (see page 97 if you need a refresher). You'll also need a rag, a small funnel, and gloves to protect your hands.

1. Locate the oil filler cap, which sits on top of the engine. It will either say "engine oil" or be marked with an oil symbol (the little oil canister with a droplet coming from its spout).

2. Remove the cap and place it in a safe spot. (People lose their caps all the time.) Place the funnel in the fill hole.

3. Add oil. Pour a quart of the oil (usually one bottle) into the funnel, taking care not to leak any oil on parts around the oil

pan. Oil can cause damage to rubber parts, so be sure to wipe up any spills. Replace the cap after the first quart.

4. Turn the engine on for a few seconds to help the oil circulate. Turn off the engine, then check the level using your dipstick.

5. Adjust. If the oil level is still too low, add another quart, repeating steps 3 and 4.

DIY #4:
How to Check and Add Coolant

Coolant leaks and overheating issues are common, especially on cars whose mileage is getting above 100,000. They can have various causes, from the radiator cracking and rubber hoses breaking down to the thermostat getting stuck. You won't necessarily be able to diagnose the underlying issue, but an awareness of your coolant level will help you make sure your engine temperature is properly regulated at all times. When should you check your coolant?

- Before going on a road trip longer than two hours

- Monthly once the car passes the 100,000-mile mark

- Weekly if you have a small coolant leak

How to Check Your Coolant

The only tool you need to check your coolant? Your eyes. But before you proceed, make sure the engine has cooled down and the car has been off for at least thirty minutes. Do not remove the radiator cap (see page 226 for location). If the engine is still hot, you could seriously injure yourself. Once the car has cooled down, pop the hood and follow two simple steps:

1. Locate your coolant reservoir, a bottle that sits close to your radiator and will be marked with the symbol of a thermostat in water. If you don't see it, look for a hose attached to the radiator, near the radiator cap; the coolant reservoir should be on the other end of that hose.

2. Read the Full/Low or Max/Min level indicators on the side of the reservoir.

If your coolant level is low, it's time to give your reservoir a refill.

Check Your Radiator Hoses

When you're checking and/or adding coolant, take the opportunity to examine your three coolant hoses. A small hose connects to your coolant reservoir, a larger hose at the top of the radiator brings hot coolant from the engine into the radiator, and another large hose at the bottom of the radiator sends cooled-off coolant from the radiator back to the engine.

You can easily reach the small hose to the reservoir and the big hose to the top of the radiator, but the bottom hose may be harder to reach and only accessible to a PCT using a lift.

When the engine and coolant are cold, grab the hoses and squeeze them. Coolant hoses that are squishy, gummy, or cracked should be replaced.

Coolant Leaks

Cars lose coolant naturally with use. But if you suspect you have a leak, take your car to your PCT right away to determine the culprit. How can you tell? Coolant is a neon color—neon pink, green, orange, or blue—so look for a neon-colored fluid around the radiator or underneath the car.

Coolant is poisonous—but that bright color and its sweet smell tend to attract kids and pets. Some coolants contain unpleasant flavoring additives to help prevent accidental poisoning, but all coolant should be kept out of reach of kids and pets. Any spills or leaks should be cleaned up with paper towels and/or kitty litter.

How to Add Coolant to Your Car

You don't need any tools to add fluids under the hood. The only thing that's nonnegotiable is the coolant (get the premixed kind, at a mix of 50/50 or 70/30 coolant to water), but you might also throw in a rag and gloves to keep things clean.

1. Park the car on level ground and turn off the engine.

2. Open the coolant reservoir cap and pour coolant into the bottle, stopping when you have reached the max level indicator on the side of the bottle. Take care not to spill coolant as you pour. Easy, right?

Under Pressure

Your engine is so hot that without a special system in place, coolant would normally boil off as soon as it came in contact with it. To prevent coolant from boiling off during normal operations, your coolant system is pressurized, increasing the coolant's boiling temperature to above 250 degrees Fahrenheit. The radiator cap is what keeps the system under 15 pounds of pressure, so ♩#shecanics must be *extremely* careful when unscrewing it. Opening a radiator cap while it is still pressurized could cause hot coolant to explode onto your face and body. The pressure drops as the coolant temperature goes down, so waiting for the engine to cool will keep you safe—and it's generally good practice for working on anything under the hood.

Some coolant reservoirs feature pressurized caps as well. If this is the case for your car, it is important that the engine and the coolant be cold before you open the cap. A pressurized cap will be marked with a warning.

Motion Electric: The Electrical Systems and Computers Inside Your Car

Early cars didn't have electrical or computer systems. A bell was used in place of an electric horn, headlights were gas lamps, and engines were started by hand. Introduced to improve the safety of those functions, electricity eventually became a component of countless operational functions (turning on the car, diagnosing failures, controlling emissions); additional safety features (lights, horns, dashboard signals, antilock brakes); and luxury amenities (radio, heat and AC, GPS, remote starters, keyless entry). As advances in technology and engineering continue to allow additional functions, the amount of electricity used to keep it all working has increased. Now electricity is also used to run a whole slew of computers and microprocessors tucked away in all corners of our cars, monitoring and tweaking everything from air bag deployment and engine function to suspension.

Diagnoses and repairs on electrical systems and computer modules can be complex. This chapter will focus on the major components of this system and the areas most likely to need maintenance, repair, or replacement.

How Batteries Work—and Why They Don't Last Forever

In modern cars, everything starts with the battery. The battery supplies the energy needed to get your engine running, then sustains an ever-expanding array of electrical functions and computerized features. To do this, batteries must generate a tremendous amount of electrical energy.

No matter the size, from the teensy batteries that run our remote controls to the super-batteries that are big as a room and control computer data centers, all batteries are born, emit electricity, and eventually die. Remember the school science experiment where you turned a lemon, a piece of copper wire, and a steel nail into a battery strong enough to power an LED bulb? What the experiment demonstrates is that you need three things to supply electricity: corrosive acid (in a lemon, that's citric acid), two dissimilar metals (steel nail and copper wire), and a device in need of electricity (LED bulb).

Inside a manufactured battery, you've got two dissimilar metal plates or posts sitting in an acid bath. One plate is copper (the positive or + plate), and the other is steel (the negative or – plate). The contact between the metal and the corrosive acid causes a chemical reaction inside the battery. And when a chemical reaction happens, electrons flow. That electron flow is electricity. Connect an

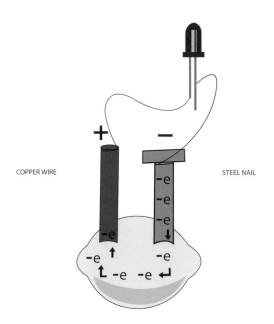

COPPER WIRE

STEEL NAIL

Copper, steel, and acid make magic, creating the same kind of reaction that happens in household and car batteries.

electricity-guzzling device to the battery, and the electrons will flow from the battery to the device, turning it on.

The reason batteries don't last forever? They contain limited quantities of acid and metal. This is true of both disposable batteries (batteries for toys and remote-controlled devices) and rechargeable models (like the ones in our cars or cell phones), and it's true of batteries of all sizes. As soon as a battery is born, a chemical reaction begins to occur. At ages one and two, the acid and metal are new, the reaction is strong, and electrons are flowing like a sink faucet turned all the way on. As the battery ages, that reaction eats up the metal and turns the acid into water (hence the reason old batteries freeze in cold weather). Once the acid and metal are all reacted, the electron flow is finished. Poof!

For a car battery, the life span is four to seven years. For that reason, make sure you buy your battery from a place that sells a lot of them and sees a bunch of foot traffic. A battery that has been sitting on the shelf for a while won't function as "new" when it is installed in your car.

Your Wheels, Your $$$: The Price of Keeping the Lights On

Electrical work is complex and generally expensive, requiring a highly skilled PCT and sometimes many hours of detective work. And it becomes even more expensive when you're dealing with luxury cars, because they are loaded up with advanced electrical systems. The price of those repairs is another thing to consider if you're in the market for a new car. See page 241 to make sure you're buying a car you can afford to maintain.

The Alternator: An Outlet for Your Car

I don't know about you, but when my smartphone charge gets down below 20 percent, I start changing my life plans in order to get to an electrical outlet. If you have a gas-powered engine, you don't have to do the same with your car.

Like a smartphone battery, a car battery is rechargeable. And just like its tinier cousin, which drains more quickly when we have lots of apps open, a car battery can be taxed by our usage patterns. Driving at night (headlights on) through the rain (windshield wipers and defrost turned on) with the radio blaring is one high-energy scenario that would drain the battery quickly. A lot of electricity is required to drive the car and power all the electronic accessories. If the car battery were the only mechanism supplying that electricity, it would drain to 0 percent in less than fifteen minutes.

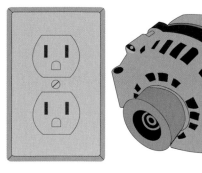

The alternator—your battery's electrical outlet.

Enter the alternator, a giant electrical outlet for your battery. You plug your phone into an electrical outlet to recharge its battery. And a car battery is plugged into the alternator with a thick wire. But the alternator doesn't just keep the battery fully charged. It also supplies all the electricity that powers the car's electronics while the engine is running. Just as the battery is plugged into the alternator (electrical outlet), so are all the car's electrical components.

Where does the alternator get its power?

From the hardworking crankshaft. As we learned on page 87 of the engine chapter, the crankshaft has lots of jobs, and powering the alternator is one of them. Once the crankshaft is spinning, the engine is running, the alternator is turned on, and all electrical, electronic, and computerized functions are powered via electricity. When the engine isn't running, the alternator is off, and the battery is no longer being charged.

How to Avoid Shortening Your Battery Life

Did you know your battery is working even while your car is parked? Even when the key isn't in the ignition, the battery powers several small electronic components through parasitic draw—your car's radio, computers, internal lights, and various other functions that continue to operate long after you've shut down the engine. And with the engine turned off, the alternator isn't running, so the battery is feeding all of these functions without being recharged. Luckily none of these functions requires a lot of electrical power. But leave your lights on overnight with your engine off, and you will kill your battery dead. You'll need a jump-start to get moving again.

Same goes for leaving your car parked for too long. The battery will slowly lose charge, and eventually you'll need a jump in order to regain enough charge to start.

That's not the end of the world, and we'll learn how to jump-start a car on page 283. But every time we drain our batteries and jump them, we shorten their lives. We can also do this by leaving headlights, internal lights, or radios on overnight, or by ignoring electrical issues that cause excessive parasitic draw (we'll learn more about these in a moment).

Generally, car batteries contain enough acid and metal to last four to seven years. Excessive heat can shorten the life of a battery, so it's worth getting your PCT to check yours if it's hovering around the four-year mark and you've just gone through a particularly hot summer. Batteries don't like to start in cold winter temperatures, either, so an older, tired battery will tend to give out just when it's least convenient for you—in the freezing cold, when all you want to do is get in your car and set the heaters on blast. (Remember, the chemical reaction produces water. The older the battery, the more water it contains, and the higher the risk that the water will freeze in cold weather.)

Your PCT can test your battery's condition for you, but here are some symptoms of a weak battery:

- Weak or dim headlights

- Weak or dim internal lights

- Slow start

Follow these tips to avoid running your battery down:

- Make sure all your internal and external lights are off when you turn off the engine.

- Don't leave the lights or radio on for long periods of time without the engine running.

- Arrange for someone to run your engine once or twice a month for fifteen minutes when you don't drive your car for a prolonged period.

- Unplug your phone charger when your car is turned off. Even if it's not plugged into your phone, the charger is drawing juice from the battery.

The Starter: A Mini-Motor for Your Crankshaft

A small but powerful electrical motor mounted to your engine, the starter (you guessed it) has starting your engine as its entire job. This component connects the battery and the engine's crankshaft, drawing energy from the battery to begin the crankshaft's rotation.

How does it work? When you turn the key in the ignition, a signal is sent to the battery to send electricity to the starter motor. That electrical surge turns on the starter motor and pops out a small spinning gear. The gear catches on the crankshaft (that's the *chug-chug-chug* you hear when you start the car) and sets the entire whirligig into motion. As soon as the crankshaft is rotating, the starter motor disengages its gear, which pops back inside the starter. The engine begins to run on fuel, air, and spark as the Eat, Burn, Belch cycle commences.

Now the starter kicks back in the off position, waiting until it's time for you to start the car again.

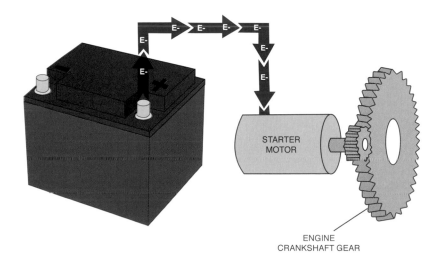

STARTER MOTOR

ENGINE CRANKSHAFT GEAR

The Fuse Box: Command Central for the Electrical System

Located under your hood, the fuse box contains fuses and switches just like the circuit breakers inside your house. Its components protect the battery's electrical wiring from overheating caused by electrical surges, and in some fuse boxes, switches called relays help direct all that energy to its proper destination. Fuses come in all sizes and ratings, depending on the size of the wiring they're protecting, but the most common are in the 7.5A to 40A range. The *A* stands for *amps,* which is short for *amperes,* a measurement of the speed at which electrical current flows. The higher the amps, the more electron flow, the more electricity, the thicker the wire. This is why battery cable wires are thick, while radio wires are thin.

TIP: *Before replacing a fuse, your PCT should come up with a diagnosis of what caused it to blow. A fuse usually blows because the wire it is protecting is faulty or an electrical component is failing. Just replacing the fuse may not prevent the problem from happening again.*

If an electrical component in your car isn't working, your mechanic will likely check the fuses first.

Headlights, Taillights, Turn Signals, and More

The lights in our homes are generally connected to outlets or to wiring embedded in our walls. In our cars, most of the lights are plugged into the battery—and that means everything from headlights and interior dome lights to the lights on your dash. When the engine is on, the battery is being fed by the alternator, and life is good. There's enough power to go around. When the engine is off, any working lights are feeding directly off the battery. And by now you know what that means. Check your lights to be sure they're off before you park for the night.

Like any lightbulbs, the bulbs in your car will eventually blow out. Depending on the car, changing a blown-out headlight or taillight bulb can be an easy DIY fix or a job for your mechanic. Do an Internet search for the bulb you need to change and the year, make, and model of your car, and you'll probably find a video showing you exactly how to replace the light. If it looks doable, work that #shecanic mojo!

Another tip: Keeping spare headlight and taillight bulbs in your glove box is a great idea. Cops *will* pull you over and ticket you for driving with a taillight out.

Your Computer on Wheels

Today's cars are smarter, safer, and more efficient than ever. And self-driving cars with the potential to dramatically reduce the number of accidents on the road are said to be just around the corner.

But the net result of all this innovation is that our cars have become more and more saturated with technology.

Whether a highway full of driverless vehicles is just a few years away or a futurist's far-off fantasy, the network of computers, controls, sensors, switches, and wires inside the average car today is already incomprehensible to the average person. So to keep things simple, we're going to cover only the high-tech components most likely to fail from use over time.

> **Powertrain Control Module (PCM).** *Module* is basically just another word for *computer,* and this one covers more than one hundred parts and functions in the average car, managing sensors, switches, and other controls that monitor and measure all functions related to the powertrain. That includes air, fuel, lubrication, exhaust, and emissions, as well as the overall condition of the engine, transmission system, and accessories. The module communicates any issues it detects by illuminating the check-engine light and/or a more specific message on your dash. In older cars, functions are regulated by separate engine control, transmission control, and body control modules (the ECM, TCM, and BCM). In newer cars, the PCM controls it all.

> **Steering Control Module.** The steering control module manages the sensors, switches, and other controls that monitor and measure steering conditions—and sometimes makes vital adjustments that prevent a crash. When the module detects issues, it will illuminate the power steering symbol on your dash.

> **Suspension Control Module.** In cars with electronic suspension systems, the suspension control module manages sensors, switches, and other controls that monitor suspension

conditions. This module provides a firm suspension for fast cornering and quick acceleration and braking, along with a soft ride for cruising. When the module detects issues, it will illuminate the suspension symbol on your dash.

Brake Control Module. The brake control module manages sensors, switches, and other controls that monitor braking conditions—and sometimes makes adjustments that prevent a crash, helping you maintain control over your vehicle. When the module detects issues, it illuminates the brake, antilock braking system (ABS), or electronic stability control (ESC) dashboard lights.

Climate Control Module. In cars with electronic interior temperature controls, the climate control module monitors temperature.

Safety Module. The safety module monitors the function of seat belts and air bags, in some cases detecting factors such as whether a person is heavy enough to be sitting in the front passenger seat and turning off the air bag if the passenger does not meet weight requirements. When the module detects an issue, it will illuminate the air bag or seat-belt indicators on your dash.

Onboard Diagnostics and the Dreaded Check-Engine Light

Each of the networks we just learned about is constantly collecting information about the various processes going on in your car. When there's an issue, the modules tell the driver about it through simple dashboard symbols or messages. If one of those signals is the check-engine light, you'll take your car to your PCT so that he or she can communicate with your car's powertrain control module on a whole other level.

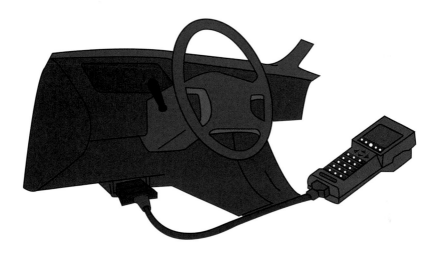

Using what's called a diagnostic scan tool, your PCT will plug into a port called an OBD (onboard diagnostics) connector, which spits out trouble codes and live data about your car. These codes give your PCT hints about what could be causing the check-engine light to illuminate. Remember, the check-engine light illuminates when the powertrain control module detects a problem in any of the air, fuel, lubrication, exhaust, and emissions systems that could be causing you to burn fuel inefficiently.

There are hundreds of trouble codes, so this is where things get tricky. Along with electrical issues in general, the diagnosis and repair of a problem triggering the check-engine light can be a particularly challenging corner of auto repair, and for this reason it is sometimes time-consuming and expensive. Best-case scenario, the issue is something as simple as the gas cap being loose. Worst case, you're up for an expensive repair. But the costs may rise if you continue to drive without addressing the problem.

As we discussed back in the dashboard chapter, static check-engine lights shouldn't cause you to panic or pull over right away. Driving a car with a static check-engine light on isn't unsafe, but it does mean that you are burning fuel inefficiently (you may actually notice that you are using more gas) or that you're spewing extra pollution into the environment (which you *won't* notice unless it's really bad, in which case your exhaust will be black and smelly).

If your check-engine light comes on, take your car to your PCT ASAP for a diagnosis. Can't afford to fix the issue? Ask your mechanic how long you can put off the repair without compromising on safety or causing further damage to your car.

WARNING: *If your check-engine light is flashing, take your car in to your PCT immediately or call for a tow if you can't get to a mechanic within five to ten minutes. Do not procrastinate. Continuing to drive with a flashing check-engine light could cause damage to the engine or other parts of the car.*

ELECTRICAL MAINTENANCE AND REPAIRS

PART	ISSUE	FIX	TIMING	COST
Battery	All batteries will eventually use up the acid and metal they contain	Replace	Normally functioning batteries last four to seven years	Less than $150 for battery and installation
Battery Posts, Terminal, and Cables	As batteries age, corrosion causes a greenish-white powder to build up on terminals and cables. Corrosion can cause a poor connection and eventually failure to start, and/or make it difficult for the alternator to charge the battery; terminals may need to be replaced	A quality PCT will take care of this problem by cleaning off the corrosion and spraying the terminals with a corrosion protectant. The DIY fix? Brush off the powder with a tooth-brush dipped in a baking soda and water solution. (Some people pour cola over the terminal to remove corrosion— and it actually works.) Take the opportu-nity to make sure that cables are tightened snugly onto the terminals and the battery is held down tightly to the frame	As needed	$15–$30 to have the battery cleaned

PART	ISSUE	FIX	TIMING	COST
Battery Hold-Down Parts	Car batteries are tightly held down to the frame of the car by brackets that prevent internal damage from vibration and movement. These brackets and their hardware can rust, and the bolts can loosen over time	Check or have your PCT check to make sure brackets are secure. Replace any worn parts or hardware	Annually	Less than $50 to replace
Sensors and Switches	Sensors and switches will fail from use over time or from excessive heat to the wires	Replace	These parts can go at any time	Varies greatly; prices may range from $5 to $1,000 depending on the location of the part and how difficult it is to access
Starter or Alternator	The starter or alternator will sometimes fail without warning, most likely creating the need for a tow. Battery problems can also be a sign of an impending alternator failure	Replace	Both of these parts normally start to fail after 80,000 miles	The parts themselves are expensive (about $350), but the labor is normally simple and quick. Tip: You can save money by buying a refurbished alternator and starter, but make sure they come with a warranty

PART	ISSUE	FIX	TIMING	COST
Electronic Components, Controls, and Computer Modules	Failure of computers and/or electronic accessories (radios, GPS system, power windows, and more) can be due to wiring issues causing surges, inherent problems, or wear over time	Varies from repairing wiring to replacing the affected part	These parts can go at any time	Can require a lot of detective work, depending on the issue, on top of the part and labor; costs may be high, especially on luxury cars
Electrical Wiring and Connectors	Wires fail from electrical surges, excessive heat, corrosion, and wear	Varies, depending on wiring and parts involved	These parts can go at any time	Can require a lot of detective work to chase down the wires and connectors affected; costs may be high, especially on luxury cars

Your Wheels, Your $$$: The Bells and Whistles

Computers, modules, radios, GPS systems, digital heating and AC controls, power windows . . . The more electronic accessories on a car, the more likely you are to have to pay for a repair when one of them fails. What needs to be replaced? Computers and modules tend to be reliable, but electronic parts (particularly sensors) *can* fail. The most common causes of failure in electronic components are use over time and poor wire connections. The latter can lead to zapping (aka shorting or killing) of the component due to an excessive electrical surge. So beware of splurging for those bells and whistles when buying a car—you may end up having to pay for them twice.

The Tricky Business of Diagnosing Electrical Wire Failure

Whenever a vehicular component that requires electricity fails, most car owners assume that the problem lies with the component. If the heater fails, it must be the blower motor, right? But sometimes the wiring that connects the blower motor to the electrical source, the alternator, is the point of failure. This is where things can get tricky. A blown fuse, a misbehaving switch, and a part malfunction are all issues that could be linked to a wire failure.

To diagnose the issue, your PCT will need to track down the bad wires and replace or repair them. No small task, given that there is more than one mile of wire inside a modern car. We could spend all week trying to find the problem, especially on a luxury car, so be patient. The right PCT will eventually get there.

One last thing: Adding aftermarket electronic systems or parts such as remote start functions, car radios, and TVs can wreak havoc on wiring; a trusted third party (not the auto manufacturer) will need to tie in to the car's electronic system to add these features.

Electric Cars

Though electric cars make up less than 1 percent of the cars on the road today, they've been around since the 1830s. But with the current enthusiasm for energy independence, the electric movement is gaining momentum. Here's a look at some of the pros and cons.

On the plus side, electric cars:

+ Do not emit pollutants. Their engines are powered not by gasoline but by several batteries.

+ Do not make as much noise as gas-powered cars. This sounds appealing but can also be dangerous, since people (especially children) don't hear them coming down the road.

+ Help reduce our dependence on foreign oil.

+ Generate tax incentives for drivers.

+ Require less maintenance and repair. Electric engines fail less often than gas engines because all they require is electric current traveling through wires; they don't need fuel, coolant, oil, spark plugs, gaskets, seals, and all the other parts involved in getting a gas engine to work.

On the downside:

- Repairs will be expensive. You'll need to find a reputable dealer qualified to work on electric cars—most independent shops and chains handle only standard vehicles.

- Many cars can get around 80 percent charged in half an hour using public rapid chargers, but recharging a battery using a regular charger can take six to eight hours.

- You'll have to plan your routes carefully when driving long distances in order to ensure access to places where you can charge up again.

- Electric cars are more expensive at purchase than gas-powered cars.

The Hybrid Road

Here's my bid on hybrids, the split-personality wonders outfitted with both a small gasoline engine *and* an electric engine. Large batteries supply power to an electrical engine, and a small gas engine acts as backup, kicking in and helping out when the car needs more power than the battery can supply.

Though they haven't quite taken over like the industry predicted they would, there are a good number of hybrid cars on the road today.

While hybrids are more expensive at purchase, they don't require any maintenance beyond what a regular gas-powered car needs. The routine maintenance and minor repairs are not more expensive on a hybrid, and they may actually be cheaper. However, if something goes wrong with the car's hybrid system after its warranty has expired, you could be charging up that credit card. Hybrid repairs are expensive and require specialized PCTs, not least because the batteries in hybrids are extremely powerful and capable of delivering fatal electric shocks. (The high-voltage wires on a hybrid have orange covers to alert any person working on the car of the danger.)

Since hybrids cost more to buy and more to repair than standard cars of similar size, does the higher gas mileage really save money in the long haul? The answer depends on factors such as the price of gas, how much you drive, and how long you keep the car. One thing you'll know for sure is that if you decide to buy a hybrid, you can feel good about helping the environment.

Signs of a Battery, Starter, or Alternator Issue

PROBLEM: Battery keeps draining and needs a jump every time you turn the car on.

CAUSE: Weak battery in need of replacement, or alternator in need of replacement.

PROBLEM: Car shuts down and loses all electrical power while driving. Sometimes all the dashboard lights illuminate before the car shuts off.

CAUSE: Alternator in need of replacement.

PROBLEM: Battery dashboard light is illuminated.

CAUSE: A red light means the battery isn't being charged. Check the alternator and the serpentine belt.

PROBLEM: Headlights or interior lights are dim.

CAUSE: Poor connections at battery posts and cable, or weak battery in need of replacement.

PROBLEM: Car won't start, with audible clicking or sputtering when you turn the key in the ignition.

CAUSE: Poor connections at battery posts and cable, or weak battery in need of a jump or replacement.

PROBLEM: Engine is slow to crank. You may have to hold the key in the start position for longer than usual to start the car and the *chug-chug-chug* (the sound of the starter motor turning the crankshaft) will be slow.

CAUSE: Poor connections at battery posts and cable, weak battery in need of a jump or replacement, or starter motor in need of replacement.

PROBLEM: Car won't start, makes no noise or clicking sound, but all lights turn on.

CAUSE: Poor wire connections at starter, starter in need of replacement, or weak battery.

PROBLEM: Battery will not jump-start or accept a charge.

CAUSE: Poor connections at battery posts and cable, or dead battery in need of replacement.

PROBLEM: Car won't turn over. You hear the *chug-chug-chug* of the starter motor turning the crankshaft, but then nothing happens. This means all electrical systems are working to get the engine started.

CAUSE: A fuel or air or spark delivery issue is preventing the engine from getting enough fuel, air, or spark to run.

Transmission: An Orderly Transfer of Power

Your car's battery gets things going by providing the electricity that starts the engine. The engine shows up with its powerful mini-explosions, turning on the alternator and feeding electricity to the rest of the car. Now it's time for the wheels to spin. That's when the transmission joins the party.

Like the engine, the transmission is a large, complex machine that is expensive to repair. Unlike the engine, the transmission is a low-maintenance system. Some good news, right?

If you've ever ridden a bike, you're already familiar with how your car's transmission works. A set of gears that transfers the power of the engine's mini-explosions to the wheels, the transmission (in both manual and automatic cars) operates just like the gears on your childhood bicycle. On a bike, the gears are visible—toothed wheels connected along a bike chain. They transfer the power produced by your feet on the pedals to the bike's wheels. The faster and harder you pedal, the faster the gears' rotations, and the faster the wheels on that bike spin. You switch gears to make it easier to accelerate the bike and to go up hills, moving the chain to a smaller- or larger-toothed gear depending on how you want the bike to ride.

Your car's transmission works in a very similar way, but it's housed in a big block of metal attached to the engine. Inside are gears connected to several spinning shafts that ultimately spin the wheels of your car.

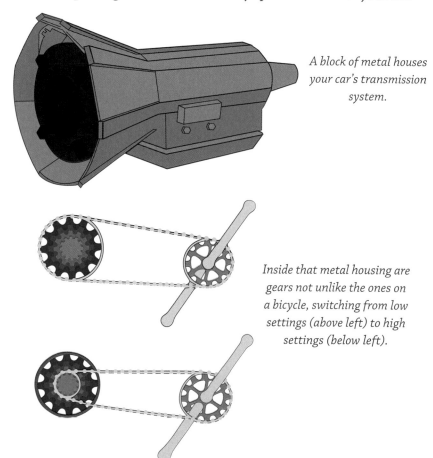

A block of metal houses your car's transmission system.

Inside that metal housing are gears not unlike the ones on a bicycle, switching from low settings (above left) to high settings (below left).

The Four Types of Transmission Systems

The type of transmission system in your car will affect the vehicle's cost, along with the frequency and cost of maintenance and repair, so you should familiarize yourself with the options.

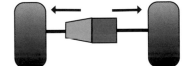

■ Engine

◣ Transmission

■ Differential

◝ Transfer case

Use this handy key to decipher the diagrams on the following pages.

The wheels the transmission connects to and spins are called the **drive wheels**. Some transmissions connect to only the front wheels of the car, while others connect to the rear. Larger trucks and SUVs have all four wheels connected to the transmission. All transmission systems use a main transmission, which is attached to the engine, and several mini transmissions or gear boxes that help direct and control the power from the engine to the wheels. These gear boxes are called differentials and transfer cases.

Front-Wheel Drive

Front-wheel drive is the type of two-wheel-drive transmission you'll find on most coupes, sedans, and minivans, as well as

Front

A single transmission is used in a FWD system— the main transmission (also called a transaxle), which is attached to the front wheels by axle shafts. The rear wheels follow along once the front wheels begin to spin.

Back

on some crossover SUVs and light trucks. This is the most basic transmission system, composed of the fewest parts and requiring the least maintenance.

+ *Pros:* The FWD transmission is the most cost-effective at purchase. It puts the driving wheels at the front of the car, giving the tires better traction, which is particularly helpful if you are driving or stuck in snow, sand, or mud. (Because the engine and transmission are located under the hood, the front of the car carries most of the car's weight—hence its improved traction.)

− *Cons:* The front tires of a front-wheel-drive vehicle do the accelerating, the steering, and most of the braking, so they wear faster than the rear tires. That annual tire rotation becomes increasingly important. Front-wheel-drive cars aren't as fun to drive if you like speed, driving around curves, and performance.

Rear-Wheel Drive

Rear-wheel drive is a two-wheel-drive transmission system found on smaller, sportier cars and two-wheel-drive trucks. Rear-wheel

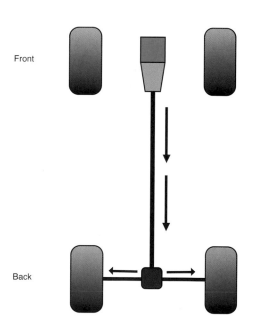

In an RWD system, the main transmission and the differential drive the rear wheels on the car together. The main transmission is attached to the two rear wheels by a driveshaft, U-joints, the differential, and axle shafts.

drive handles better around corners and for quick acceleration or braking.

+ *Pros:* Better handling in dry road conditions than an FWD transmission, and faster acceleration or "pickup." When you accelerate in any car, the weight of the vehicle shifts backward—and with RWD you've got the driving wheels picking up the slack. (The extreme version of this is a wheelie, which only a power engine can do, when the front tires lift off the ground.)

- *Cons:* More expensive at purchase. May cost more in gas. Since most of the weight of the car is in the front, the rear tires don't have as much traction as on an FWD vehicle. They do not perform as well when driving in snow, sand, or mud as an FWD. If you have an RWD vehicle, take extreme caution in poor road conditions to avoid getting stuck.

Four-Wheel Drive

Now we're getting a little fancy! Front-wheel-drive and rear-wheel-drive systems are great for coupes and sedans, but trucks and SUVs require something a little more robust. These vehicles carry heavy loads, tow cargo, and have large parts and tires that require more engine power, and that's what a 4WD transmission helps provide— along with great traction in adverse and off-road driving conditions.

+ *Pros:* Great road traction to keep you safe when driving in adverse weather conditions or off-road. More power for towing cargo or another car.

- *Cons:* More expensive to buy, maintain, and repair. Requires more gas, and more frequent tire rotations.

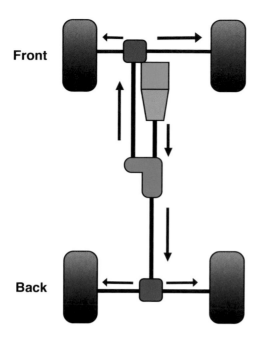

Front

Back

In a 4WD system, the main transmission, a transfer case, and two differentials (one front and one rear) drive the front and rear wheels at the same time.

Part-Time Four-Wheel Drive

A part-time four-wheel-drive transmission system doesn't need to be activated at all times. Full-time 4WD vehicles are also known as AWD vehicles, covered in the following section; part-time 4WD systems have you switching between 2WD and 4WD, and between high and low gears, depending on the circumstances. Here's how and when to use each.

- 2WD High, aka 2H, 2Hi: During normal driving conditions. Essentially allows the car to run on an RWD transmission system.

- 4WD High, aka 4H, 4Hi: If you need more traction when driving in ice, snow, sand, or other common off-road conditions.

- 2WD Low, aka 2L, 2Lo, or 2Low: If you are towing something heavy.

- 4WD Low, aka 4L, 4Lo, or 4Low: If you are towing something heavy in ice, snow, or sand, or if you are driving in extreme off-road conditions.

In part-time 2WD, the transmission reverts to rear-wheel drive, with the transfer case spinning only the rear differential and rear wheels.

All-Wheel Drive

Once limited to Subarus, AWD transmission systems are popping up on average cars everywhere. Now some sedans and many SUVs and trucks come equipped with AWD transmissions. An AWD vehicle is essentially running in 4WD High (useful if you need more traction, when driving in ice, snow, or sand, or other common off-road conditions) at all times.

+ *Pros:* Better handling around corners. Great in all driving conditions, on- and off-road. Most people buy AWD vehicles specifically for off-road conditions.

- *Cons:* More expensive to buy, repair, and maintain. Should be considered a luxury item for added safety and drivability unless you live in an area that gets a lot of snow and ice. You will have to take better care of your tires and match all four tires for wear and brand. That means if you replace one worn-out tire, you'll likely have to replace all four.

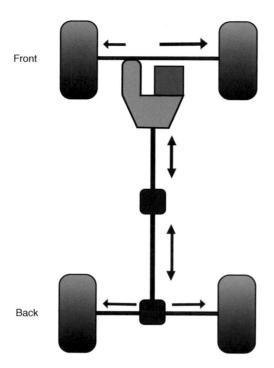

Front

Back

Most all-wheel-drive systems use the main transmission along with three differentials (situated in the front, rear, and center of the car) to drive both the *front wheels* and *the rear wheels* at the same time.

Your Wheels, Your $$$: Don't Spend Money on Unnecessary Transmission Power

If you don't live in a place that gets a lot of snow, don't need to carry large loads, and/or don't plan on driving off-road, there's really no advantage to buying an AWD or 4WD vehicle. You'll spend more up front and on maintenance and gas.

But if snow and ice are common during your winter season, you should consider buying an AWD or 4WD vehicle; *common* doesn't mean you see snow a handful of times per winter and typically get less than 3 inches.

The least expensive systems to buy, maintain, and repair, FWD transmissions are perfectly fine for coupes, sedans, minivans, or crossover SUVs, especially if you don't frequently encounter a lot of snow.

Four-Wheel Drive and All-Wheel Drive and Your Tires

A difference in diameter of less than half an inch between front and rear tires on a 4WD or AWD vehicle can mean trouble for your transmission system. And as tire tread wears down, tires shrink. A new tire is rounder (and therefore taller) than a tire that has been driven for many miles. A bigger, newer tire travels more distance in a single revolution than a smaller, used tire. So to compensate, a smaller-diameter tire will spin faster than a bigger-diameter tire. On a 4WD or AWD vehicle, heat buildup from a smaller tire spinning faster can cause stress to axles, shafts, joints, and differentials, also confusing the systems that monitor transmission and wheel speed. The powertrain control module may think that the transmission is slipping or that conditions are snowy or rainy, and automatically shift gears or adjust the transmission.

For this reason, when a tire needs to be replaced on a 4WD vehicle, it is best practice to replace the tire on the opposite side as well, and to match tire brand while you're at it. If a tire needs to be replaced on an AWD vehicle, it is more than likely that you must replace all four tires.

Check your owner's manual or call your PCT to find out. Ignoring this advice may result in costly damage to some of the most important driving components of your car, including the transmission.

TRANSMISSION MAINTENANCE AND REPAIRS

PART	ISSUE	FIX	TIMING	COST
Automatic Transmission Fluid	Not maintaining the automatic transmission fluid as needed can cause hard shifting or slipping—when the gears inside the transmission aren't catching as they shift. While driving, it will feel like the car wants to speed up as you press on the gas pedal, but it will hesitate before the gear catches and the car accelerates. If you can check the transmission fluid, it will smell like burned crayons when your system is in need of a flush	On some vehicles, needs very occasional fluid flushes and filter changes	See your owner's manual, but we're talking once every five to ten years	For most cars $250 or less
Differential Oil or Fluid	Oil or fluid breaks down over time, creating wear on the transmission's gears	Oil or fluid may need an occasional change-out	See your owner's manual	For most vehicles $150 or less
Main Transmission	Transmissions will fail if they are poorly driven or maintained. Some just fail from use over time. One classic way that all of us hurry up and-wait types wear out our transmissions is by trying to accelerate faster than our cars' engine power can manage	If the car won't shift, doesn't drive in reverse or in drive, or exhibits extreme slipping, the transmission will likely need replacing	Variable	Expect to spend at least $2,000 to replace a failed main transmission with a used model

PART	ISSUE	FIX	TIMING	COST
Constant Velocity (CV) Axle Shafts and CV Joints	Located on the front of the vehicle to connect the main transmission to the wheels; CV axle shafts attach to the wheel bearings and fail from use over time. The point of failure most often seen is the CV joint boot, a rubber covering designed to keep dirt and air from damaging the lubricated joints	A PCT will replace a CV axle shaft when the boot is torn or ripped; if the joint fails, the shaft will need to be replaced	When a CV axle shaft needs to be replaced, you will hear thumping noises coming from the wheels	Often, used CV axles can be installed for some savings, but make sure they come with a warranty. Less than $350 per wheel
Driveshafts and U-Joints	Driveshafts and U-joints on 4WD and AWD vehicles will fail from use over time, from corrosion, or from driver abuse (accelerating too quickly, not replacing tires in pairs or sets); U-joints often make bumping noises when going from drive to reverse or vice versa when they need to be replaced, with the sound coming from under the car seats	Replace; sometimes the driveshaft will simultaneously need to be replaced	Varies depending on what needs to be replaced	$500+

PART	ISSUE	FIX	TIMING	COST
Differentials	Differentials on 4WD and AWD vehicles will fail if they are not properly maintained. Signs of failure include grinding noises from the rear of the car while cruising or turning	When a rear differential needs to be replaced, the entire rear axle or rear end (including the differential and axle shafts) will have to be replaced as well	Variable	Greater than $1,000
Transfer Case	Transfer cases don't normally fail, unless they aren't properly maintained through occasional automatic transmission fluid flushes (see page 71) or suffer from driver abuse	Replace	Variable	Greater than $1,000
Clutch	On manual (aka stick-shift) transmissions, the clutch will wear out from use over time and from driver abuse, and the car will slip when you try to shift gears	Replace	If driven well, a clutch will last 100,000 miles or more and may need to be replaced only once during a car's lifetime	Clutch replacement is an involved job, requiring removal of the transmission; greater than $750

Common Auto Airhead Mistakes: Transmission

Transmission systems may be low-maintenance, and you gotta love 'em for that. But a transmission issue is a real pain and quite an expense, so avoid the following common mistakes to keep yours in tip-top condition:

- Ignoring problems during acceleration and when shifting gears.

- Failing to maintain the automatic transmission fluid and differential fluids. Failing to flush the automatic transmission fluid can cause hard shifting, slipping, and damage to the differentials and transmission.

- Incorrectly using part-time 4WD.

- Failing to replace tires properly on vehicles with AWD transmission systems.

- Failing to rotate tires at least once a year.

- Driving a four-cylinder engine like it's a V-6. Ease up on that gas pedal, speed demons.

Brakes: The Most Important System in Your Car

Now it's time to get down to business about what might be the most important system in your entire vehicle: the miracle of engineering that prevents a 4,000-pound car from crashing into another car, person, or tree. Slowing down or stopping a moving object of that weight takes a lot of force, much more than our little bodies and right feet can generate. It involves physics, and processes like energy, gravity, friction, and hydraulics (a fancy word for moving a liquid around to do work).

Brake Repair Time Line

The most common questions I see online are about how often drivers should replace their brakes. There's no definitive answer—because it all depends on how you drive. If you live in a city or a suburban area and often drive in stop-and-go traffic, you'll need to replace your brake pads and other parts of your brake system more frequently than if you drive mostly highway miles. On the highway, you're braking less, so the pads and other parts of the brake system don't wear as fast. Either way, brakes give you lots of audible and palpable feedback about their condition, so they will let you know when it's time to replace them, even if nothing surfaces during your regular maintenance checkup. Brakes often last at least two years, unless you drive for a living.

Front brakes, especially on front-wheel-drive vehicles, wear at a quicker rate than rear brakes, both because the engine and transmission weigh down the front of the car and because the weight of the car and its cargo shifts forward as you brake.

One way to make a DIY assessment of the condition of your brakes is to check your brake fluid (see page 172 for instructions). Your brake system is a closed system, meaning the fluid stays inside and is not affected by any outside forces or matter (air, other fluids). That means if the brake fluid is low, you don't add fluid. Low brake fluid is an indication that you need new brake pads (more likely) or you have a leak (less likely). If it's the former, new brake pads or shoes with thicker friction material will cause brake fluid levels to rise back to full. Do not top off your brake fluid!

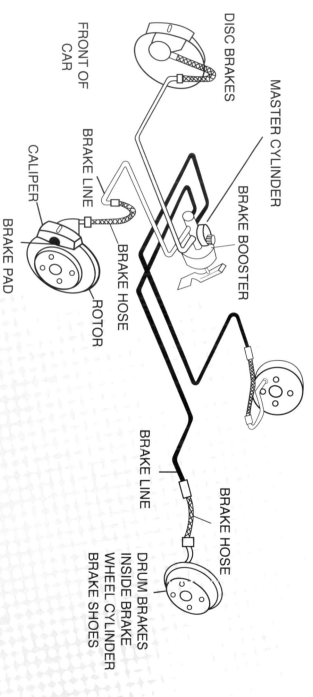

MASTER CYLINDER

DISC BRAKES

FRONT OF
CAR

BRAKE BOOSTER

BRAKE LINE

CALIPER

BRAKE HOSE

BRAKE PAD

ROTOR

BRAKE LINE

BRAKE HOSE

DRUM BRAKES
INSIDE BRAKE
WHEEL CYLINDER
BRAKE SHOES

The intricate brake system recruits hydraulic power and friction to generate the force required to slow or stop a car.

The Parts and Processes of a Brake System

There are lots of little actions going on between the moment you hit the brake pedal and the slowdown at the wheels. Here's a snapshot of the parts and processes involved. Follow along on the big picture illustration (opposite) to get a sense of how it all comes together.

Pedal. The central command station for the braking system, the pedal is set off by your foot applying force to it.

Brake Booster. It takes at least 800 and up to 2,000 pounds of pressure to slow down a 4,000-pound car. Humans need an assist, and fortunately the brake pedal is connected to a gadget called a booster. For you Super Mario Bros. fans, a brake booster is a mushroom that powers you up to a bigger, stronger Mario or Princess Peach, doubling the force generated by your foot. Most standard cars have vacuum boosters, while luxury cars have what's called a hydraulic booster. Either way, boosters involve complex engineering and aren't common points of failure.

Hydraulic System. Once it leaves the pedal, the boosted force initiated by your foot connects with a gadget under the hood called a **master cylinder**, topped by the plastic reservoir that holds your brake fluid. Boosted force pushes that fluid into the master cylinder and through the metal brake lines (pictured opposite), then down to each wheel.

Wheel Brakes. Most cars come with **disc brakes** at all four wheels, but some cars have disc brakes at the front wheels and **drum brakes** in the rear (see opposite).

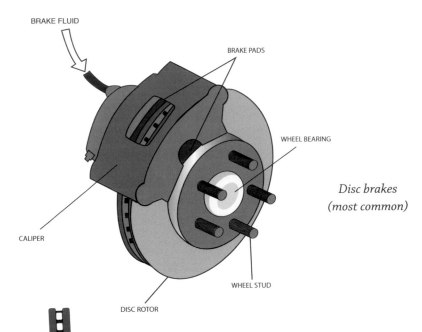

BRAKE FLUID

BRAKE PADS

WHEEL BEARING

CALIPER

WHEEL STUD

DISC ROTOR

*Disc brakes
(most common)*

*Side view of
a rotor*

With disc brakes, boosted braking force comes in contact with a **caliper**, which squeezes or clamps **brake pads** against a spinning **rotor**—a flat metal disc attached to the car's wheels. The caliper straddles the rotor and houses the brake pads.

The friction caused by contact between nonmoving parts (the brake pads) and a moving object (the rotor) causes the spinning rotor to slow down and eventually stop. Because the rotor is attached to the wheel, when the rotor slows down, the wheel slows down.

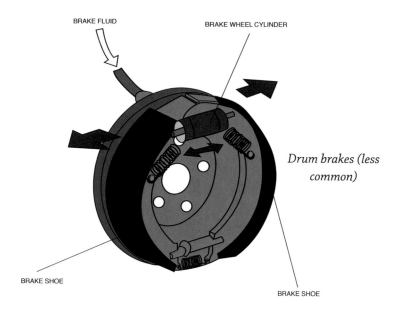

BRAKE FLUID

BRAKE WHEEL CYLINDER

Drum brakes (less common)

BRAKE SHOE

BRAKE SHOE

   With drum brakes, boosted force comes in contact with
a **wheel cylinder**, which pushes **brake shoes** up and out
against a **rotating drum**. Drum brakes work very similarly to
disc brakes—using friction to slow down a spinning wheel—
but their components are housed inside that round drum,
and metal springs are used to hold the shoes in place.

Friction Materials: *The brake pads, rotors, shoes, and drums used to
slow down the spinning wheels on your car all fall into a category of
parts called* friction materials. *They accomplish their work through
the use of friction—and like any two materials that are rubbed
against each other repeatedly (which is how you generate friction),
they will wear or deteriorate over time. Friction materials are meant
to be replaced, because wear and tear are inevitable results of their
function. So don't grumble about having to get them swapped out
or unfairly place blame on your car or your mechanic.*

   *Made of metal, rotors are a lot more durable than brake pad
material, so they don't wear away as fast. But if you wait too long
to replace your brake pads, all the friction material on the pads will
wear away. You will have a metal (brake-pad backing) on metal
(rotor) situation that results in a grinding sound and a wearing-
down of the expensive rotor. The surface of the metal rotor will be
scored with scratches, deep grooves, and general roughness.*

light wear
12mm - 8mm

moderate wear
6mm - 4mm

service soon
3mm - 2mm

When brake pads wear down to 2–3 mms, it's time to have them replaced.

The Miracle of ABS

Given everything that's going on when you press on the brake pedal, it's no wonder brake systems are loaded up with a slew of computers and sensors. There are switches that illuminate your rear brake lights, sensors that monitor brake fluid level, and valves that ensure boosted force is evenly distributed to each wheel.

Some of these sensors are designed to override our instincts. We tend to slam on our brakes when we're faced with close calls, for instance—if we're trying to avoid a crash, if the car begins to slide, or if we lose control due to poor traction between our tires and a wet or icy road. But slamming down on that pedal as you skid out of control only makes matters worse. When you panic-brake, you overtax the valves that monitor boosted force and spread that force evenly to the wheels. And if one or more of the wheels experiences a surplus of force, the brake pads and caliper clamp down harder on that wheel. The wheel will spin slower or even stop spinning entirely. This is called wheel lockup, and it can cause the car to slide or skid as the other wheels continue to spin.

In the best-case scenario, the antilock braking system and the wheel-speed sensors at each wheel will come to the rescue before then. Preventing tires from locking up during panic braking and/or braking in wet or icy weather conditions, the ABS function is a requirement on all cars made after 2013. How does it work? The ABS system is outfitted with computers and sensors of its own. At each tire, a wheel-speed sensor spits out a measurement to a computer that compares speed among all four wheels. If the computer detects an inconsistency, it will send a signal to remove boosted brake force from the slower wheel or wheels by stopping your foot from fully depressing the pedal. Reducing pressure on the brake pedal goes against all of our intuitions, but that's what the ABS system does for us by applying and releasing force from the brake pad very, very quickly. When the system engages, you'll feel the brake pedal suddenly jam up and start vibrating. That's the result of the ABS system pumping the brakes in fractions of a second, automatically achieving the pulse-style braking that will free up a locked wheel and allow you to remain in control.

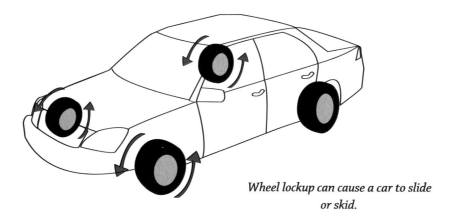

Wheel lockup can cause a car to slide or skid.

Driving Without ABS

The automatic braking system is a wonderful safety feature, but you won't be damaging your car if you drive while the system isn't working. If the ABS system is malfunctioning and you need to come to a sudden stop, try to apply pulse-style braking (aka pumping the brakes) rather than slamming all the way down on the brakes. Use your foot to tap the brake pedal lightly and quickly. Rapidly applying and releasing force to your wheels will cause the caliper and brake pads to release their clamp on the locked wheel.

Traction Control

ABS is great for helping to prevent the car from sliding during braking. Traction control (TC) and electronic stability control (ESC), also known as vehicle stability control (VSC), help control the car during acceleration, actually slowing it down when you are pulling a dangerous move. If you are taking a corner too fast and are in danger of spinning off the road and/or toppling over, these systems' sensors and computers will slow your car down automatically to prevent you from spinning out or flipping over. Often the TC and/or ESC dashboard lights (an icon of a car with wavy lines behind its tires) will illuminate while the functions are activated.

Another nice thing about traction control: The system doesn't require any maintenance. When it experiences a fault or failure, the TC dashboard light will flash.

BRAKE SYSTEM MAINTENANCE AND REPAIRS

PART	ISSUE	FIX	TIMING	COST
Brake Fluid	As it cycles through temperature changes, brake fluid gets grimy from chemical breakdown. Dirty fluid has a lower boiling point and begins to evaporate at the high temperatures common within your brake system. Evaporation leads to low brake fluid level, which will cause poor braking and could lead to a crash. Dirty brake fluid also causes corrosion of your brake parts and brake lines	Have your PCT drain and replace your brake fluid (aka brake exchange or fluid flush)	Every three to five years per your PCT's recommendation	Less than $250
Brake Pads	Material will start to wear away as your pads rub against the metal rotors	Replace	The brake pads need to be replaced when they are down to 2 millimeters or $\frac{2}{32}$ of an inch thick. Some cars have indicators on the pads that squeal to tell you when it's time, and luxury brands tend to have sensors that illuminate a light on your dash	Look to spend about $150 per axle to replace your brake pads

PART	ISSUE	FIX	TIMING	COST
Rotors	Rotors thin as they wear, and they can be further damaged by brake pads that aren't replaced in time and create scoring and circular scratches on the rotors	Replace or machine	If you change your brake pads regularly, change the rotors at every other brake pad change. Don't put new brake pads on a worn rotor, or you'll be wearing out the new pads and hearing bad braking noises in no time	Look to spend at least $350 to $500 per axle to replace both brake pads and rotors. If you need pads and rotors all around (front and rear axles), you'll be out at least $700 to $1,000
Calipers	Calipers fail from wear and tear, or if brake pads and/or rotors aren't replaced on time; failure to replace brake pads when friction material wears away will cause the calipers to overextend themselves during braking	Replace	Variable	Look to spend at least $200 to replace this expensive part at each wheel, and a little extra to bleed the brake fluid of air
Brake Shoes and Drums	The metal springs that hold the brake shoes in place need to be adjusted from time to time. You'll feel a soft or low brake pedal or hear squeaking when the springs need a tweak. Brake shoes and drums will also wear over time	Replace	Replace brake shoes when worn, about once every five to seven years or 50,000 miles; replace drums on every other brake shoe change, along with rotors. (Depending on how long you keep your car, you may never need to replace your brake drums.)	Look to spend an average of $150 to replace each brake shoe and $350 to $500 to replace both a shoe and a drum

PART	ISSUE	FIX	TIMING	COST
Wheel Cylinders	The wheel cylinders in drum brakes will fail from normal wear and tear, or if the brake shoes aren't replaced as needed. Not replacing the brake shoes when all friction material has worn away will cause the wheel cylinders to overextend themselves during braking	If the wheel cylinder on the right rear tire fails, the left rear wheel cylinder isn't far behind, so mechanics often replace wheel cylinders in pairs, and the brake fluid will also need to be bled	Variable	Look to spend at least $150 for a pair of wheel cylinders
Master Cylinder	The master cylinder will fail from use over time	Replace; brake fluid will need to be bled	Variable	Less than $750
Brake Booster	The brake booster will fail from use over time. The pedal will be too hard to push down when the booster fails	Replace	Variable	Around $500

PART	ISSUE	FIX	TIMING	COST
Brake Lines	Brake lines often fail from corrosion caused by brake fluid and/or salt exposure and will leak brake fluid until they are replaced	Replace; brake fluid will need to be bled	Variable	Price varies depending on the number of brake lines that need to be replaced. The lines themselves are inexpensive, but the job is labor-intensive; $350 and up
Vacuum Hoses	The hoses that vacuum air from the engine into the brake booster can come loose or wear from use—without the boost, you'll feel a hard brake	Attach the hoses back in place with hose clamps or replace if necessary	Variable	Less than $100
Antilock Braking System	If your car has antilock braking, each tire will be outfitted with a wheel speed sensor and metal "tone ring" that measure how fast that wheel is spinning. The sensors and rings are common points of failure, especially on pothole-ridden roads	Replace the individual points of failure	When an ABS warning dashboard light comes on and stays lit	Look to spend at least $100 per wheel

Machining vs. Replacing

You may have heard the term *machining, turning,* or *cutting* tossed around your local auto shop, but when it comes to rotors, most places don't "machine" them anymore. As with so many modern parts and appliances, the cost of a new rotor has become less than the cost of the labor involved in machining one. Drums can also be machined, but they've become just as cheap to buy new.

Parking Brake

Also called the *emergency brake*, the parking brake is a backup system applied independently of the primary brakes. It can be used in case of an emergency, but it is designed to hold a parked vehicle in place. Unless you have a manual transmission, you don't need to use the parking brake every time you park the car. If you drive an automatic and don't frequently park on hills, use the parking brake a few times a month to prevent it from getting rusty and lonely. On some cars when the parking brake is on or engaged, the parking brake *and* the brake dashboard light will be illuminated.

Signs of a Brake Issue

You should be able to hear or feel the most common signs of a brake issue. None of these should be ignored.

PROBLEM: Squealing

CAUSE: A squealing noise is an intentional indicator that brake pads need to be replaced. Brake pads come with metal indicator attachments that rub on the rotor when the pad material is worn down to 3 millimeters; this rubbing is what causes the squealing noise. Most luxury cars use an electrical indicator in place of the metal attachment; instead of a squealing noise, a dashboard light will appear when brake pads are low.

PROBLEM: Grinding

CAUSE: Grinding is caused by worn brake pads and rotors. If you let that squealing go on too long and the brake pad material wears away entirely, the brake pad backing will be rubbing against the metal rotor, causing grinding that sounds like a metal chain being dragged across concrete.

PROBLEM: Shaking during braking

CAUSE: Rotors get warped or "out of round," causing a vibration when you step on the brake pedal. If replacing the rotors doesn't fix the problem, the vibration may be caused by your tires. If your brake pads are pretty new, only the rotors will need to be replaced. This is the *only* time it's okay to replace rotors without replacing pads.

PROBLEM: Pulling during braking

CAUSE: If you feel the car pull or jerk to one side *as* you brake, one of your calipers may not be releasing the brake pad from the rotor. Your caliper or your brake hose may need replacing, or you may have a suspension or steering issue.

PROBLEM: Brake light on

CAUSE: No or low brake fluid. This indicator is the result of a brake fluid leak, or an urgent need to replace one or more parts of the brake system. If your brake light comes on while you are driving, pull over and check the brake fluid reservoir. (See page 173.) If there is fluid in the reservoir, drive your car to your PCT or to the closest service station; if there is no fluid in the reservoir, get the car towed to your PCT.

PROBLEM: Spongy brake pedal

CAUSE: If your brake pedal feels spongy when you press on it, there is air in your brake fluid, and the system needs to be bled.

PROBLEM: Low, soft, or sinking brake pedal

CAUSE: Brake fluid is low, brake pads or shoes may need replacing, drum brakes may need adjusting, or a brake fluid exchange is needed. If you have low brake fluid or your brake pads are worn down to 3 millimeters or less, the pedal will be soft, or easy to push, and you won't feel resistance (the brake pads clamping down on the rotors) until the pedal is almost to the floor. That half-second delay can translate into a collision.

PROBLEM: Brakes self-apply

CAUSE: If the brakes engage as if you stepped on the pedal when you didn't, you most likely have an issue with your master cylinder.

PROBLEM: Hard braking

CAUSE: If you press on the brake pedal and it won't push down at all, even when you use both feet and all your weight, your brake booster (that magical Super Mario Bros. mushroom) is failing and will need to be replaced.

DIY #5:
How to Check Brake Fluid and Power Steering Fluid

Being low on brake fluid or power steering fluid could be an indicator of a major issue in one of these vitally important systems. So in this section we're going to learn to check them both. Adding the wrong fluids to the brake fluid or power steering reservoir could cause damage to the systems, so all you'll be doing is checking the levels. If levels are low, take your car in as soon as possible to avoid a crash and/or an expensive repair. Do not continue to drive with low brake or power steering fluid.

Tools

None. All you need to check these fluids are your eyes.

Brake fluid cap

Checking Your Brake Fluid Level

Open the hood of your car and locate your brake fluid reservoir. There should be a max and min level indicator on the reservoir. If the fluid is low, you either need new brake pads or have a leak in the system. If the fluid is below the minimum level, you could find yourself without brakes while driving. Take the car to your PCT immediately.

Power steering fluid cap

Checking Your Power Steering Fluid Level

Open the hood of your car and locate your power steering fluid reservoir (see page 69). Check the max-min fluid level indicator on the reservoir or unscrew the cap to view the plastic dipstick.

Driving with power steering fluid below the minimum level could cause permanent damage to your steering system. If the fluid level is low, take the car to your PCT immediately.

Max

Min

Dipstick

Keep 'Em Rolling: Tires and Wheels

The only parts of a vehicle that come in contact with the ground, tires are a car's shoes. I like to picture mine as a pair of saucy red heels. And the good news about those heels is that, like any quality pair of footwear, they should last a long time—*if* you care for them properly. With some tires designed to drive 60,000 miles, you may have to buy replacements only once or twice over your vehicle's lifetime. But many of us skip the maintenance and repairs our tires require, costing ourselves more money in the long run. Even more important, neglecting your tires creates the potential for serious safety issues.

Anatomy of a Tire

The terms *tires* and *wheels* are often used interchangeably, but tires are tough, hollow rubber circles, and wheels are the round hunks of metal that the tires are placed over. Once tires are placed over the wheels, they are inflated to optimal pressure for safe and predictable driving.

There's a misconception that it's your brakes that stop a car. But the stopping action, set into motion by your brakes, is actually finished off by the friction between your tires' tread and the ground. That

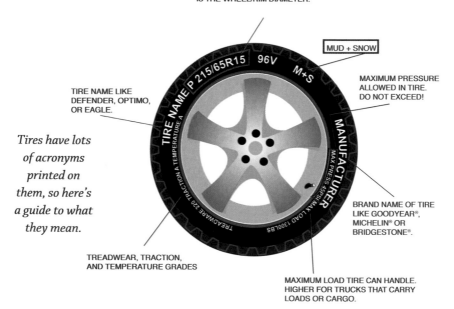

TIRE SIZE: P MEANS PASSENGER. TRUCKS MAY SAY LT FOR LIGHT TRUCK. THE NUMBER AFTER IS THE WHEEL/RIM DIAMETER.

MUD + SNOW

MAXIMUM PRESSURE ALLOWED IN TIRE. DO NOT EXCEED!

TIRE NAME LIKE DEFENDER, OPTIMO, OR EAGLE.

Tires have lots of acronyms printed on them, so here's a guide to what they mean.

BRAND NAME OF TIRE LIKE GOODYEAR®, MICHELIN® OR BRIDGESTONE®.

TREADWEAR, TRACTION, AND TEMPERATURE GRADES

MAXIMUM LOAD TIRE CAN HANDLE. HIGHER FOR TRUCKS THAT CARRY LOADS OR CARGO.

tread is super important, because it allows the tire to grip the surface of the road as you slow down. Tread also wears away over time. And when it's completely gone, your tires won't be able to effectively grip. Instead of coming to a full stop, you will come to a much slower sliding stop, a serious safety issue that could result in a crash.

The long and short of it is that driving around with bald tires is a major auto airhead mistake, but one that's easily remedied since you can actually see and assess your tire tread yourself, using the chart showing premature or uneven wear and possible causes on page 195.

Common Tire Problems and Fixes

The wheels on that bus may go 'round and 'round—but without functional tires, nobody's getting to school on time. Here are a few common issues and the fixes that will help keep you and that big yellow bus (with the fancy red heels) on schedule.

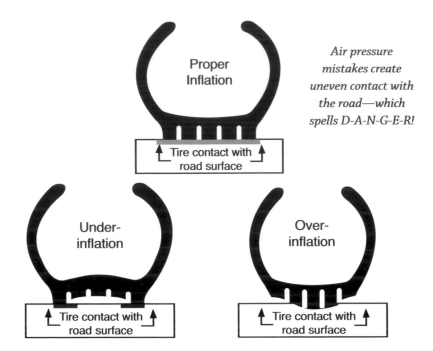

Proper Inflation

Tire contact with road surface

Air pressure mistakes create uneven contact with the road—which spells D-A-N-G-E-R!

Under-inflation

Tire contact with road surface

Over-inflation

Tire contact with road surface

Incorrect Tire Pressure

If you enjoy a smooth ride, you have the pressurized air inside your rubber tires partly to thank. But the air pressure inside those tires has got to be just right or your tire tread will wear unevenly, creating the potential for a flat. Too high, and the tread will show more wear toward the center of the tire; too low, and the sides will suffer.

You want to catch an air pressure issue long before it starts showing up on your tread, and fortunately a dashboard indicator will light up to let you know as soon as tire pressure drops to an unsafe level (about 8 psi lower than the manufacturer's recommended operation pressure). I was absolutely guilty of ignoring this symbol myself, but low tire pressure causes the following dangerous and/or money-wasting issues:

- Wastes fuel. Expensive!

- Increases braking distance. Unsafe!

- Lowers your vehicle's stability. Unsafe!

- Causes uneven wear on your tires. Expensive!

- Can cause hydroplaning or slipping on wet roads. Unsafe!

- Makes your vehicle more prone to a flat or a blowout. Unsafe *and* expensive!

When that tire pressure indicator lights up, get yourself to a gas station or to your local mechanic ASAP. A mechanic will probably do the job for you for free, and at a gas station, you'll be able to refill your tires yourself for around a dollar. You can also invest in an inexpensive portable compressor (see box, page 200) so you can refill your tires as needed without going out of your way. Unfortunately, one thing your dashboard won't tell you is that you've overfilled your tires, something I see at almost every Girls Auto Clinic car care workshop. To learn more about how to avoid making this common mistake, see page 191.

Don't Mess Around with PSI

I once got into a five-minute argument during a defensive driving course with a police officer who told us that the optimal tire pressure was marked on our tires' sidewalls. This common misconception is not only false but dangerous. The correct operating tire pressure is located on a sticker on your car's driver side doorjamb. (The average on all passenger vehicles is 33 psi.) The number on the sidewall is the *maximum* allowable air pressure in the tire.

By law, passenger cars manufactured since 2007 are equipped with tire pressure monitor systems (TPMS), a move that was a partial response to the Ford Explorer/ Firestone Tire "rollover" crashes of the 1990s. (Firestone claimed that Ford kept the tire pressures artificially low in order to stabilize the top-heavy SUVs; Ford countered that the problem was with the Firestone tires. The U.S. Congress agreed that tire pressure was at fault, and established a new Federal Motor Vehicle Safety

TIRE AND LOADING INFORMATION

| SEATING CAPACITY | TOTAL | 5 | FRONT | 2 | REAR | 3 |

The combined weight of occupants and cargo should never exceed XXX kg or XXX lbs.

TIRE	ORIGINAL SIZE	COLD TIRE PRESSURE	
FRONT	P245/50R17 98V	220kPa, 32psi	**SEE OWNER'S MANUAL FOR ADDITIONAL INFORMATION**
REAR	P245/50R17 98V	210KPa, 30psi	
SPARE	T155/70D17 110M	420kPa, 60psi	

Standard that requires the installation of a tire pressure monitoring system (TPMS) that warns the driver when a tire is significantly underinflated.

Not having the proper air pressure inside their tires is the single most common mistake drivers make. So make refilling your tires a regular part of your life. There's no standard frequency for tires needing to be refilled; waiting until the TPMS light illuminates on your dashboard is just fine. You may get a few false alarms. Because warm air expands and cold air contracts, the air pressure in a tire often drops significantly overnight, especially as seasons are changing and tires are exposed to wider ranges of outdoor temperatures. Some mornings, the tire pressure warning light will come on, but after driving for about 2 miles, the air inside the tire warms up and the TPMS light goes out. If it stays on for longer than five minutes as you drive, check your tire pressure. And be sure to measure tire pressure only after you've driven for more than 2 miles. Pro tip: It may also take a few miles of driving to turn the warning light off once you've filled the tire to the correct pressure.

TIP: *If you're driving an older car that doesn't have TPMS, check your tire pressure once a month when you fill up on gas; see page 191 for how. Seem like too much of a chore? At least take a walk around your car and have a peek at your tires. When pressure is very low, the car will droop and the tire or tires will be visibly deflated.*

Flat Tires

Flat tires aren't entirely preventable, but you're more likely to catch one if your tires are underinflated, over-inflated, and/or worn down. Maintaining proper tire pressure, rotating your tires, and replacing tires when necessary will significantly decrease your chances of catching a flat, while creating a smoother and more efficient ride. But flat tires can happen to even the most well-prepared ♪#shecanic, which is why we're going to learn how to change a tire on page 203.

Tire Leaks

If your dashboard tire pressure light reilluminates a few days after you've refilled a tire, you probably have a small leak. Check your tires again. If the same tire is low twice in a row, take your car in to your PCT. A small leak may have you refilling your tire every few days or every week, while a large leak may have you refilling your tire every day or two. Small leaks can be plugged and/or patched, an inexpensive job, whereas larger leaks will usually lead to a tire replacement.

Leaks often result from some unlucky contact between your tire and a nail or other sharp object—but they're more likely to occur on tires that are underinflated, overinflated, or worn down. (Starting to get the picture?) Leaks can also occur if the tire bead (where the rubber tire touches the metal wheel) or valve stem is broken. Faulty tire installation can cause tire bead problems, and tire valves and tire beads can also leak due to failure or rough handling.

A broken tire valve can be one cause of a leak.

Uneven Wear

In an ideal world, all four of your tires will wear evenly. That way, you'll only need to replace your full set of tires every five years or so. Uneven wear may not seem like something you can control, but it actually has four main causes, all of them avoidable.

1. Incorrect Tire Pressure. See the previous section.

2. Skipping a Scheduled Tire Rotation. Most of the car's braking is done by your front brakes, so the front tires wear out faster than the back tires. They're the car's workhorses, generating the friction that enables you to come to a stop. To boot, cars are heavier in the front, because of the engine, transmission, and all that other good stuff under the hood. More wear and tear on those front tires. That's why we have our friendly PCT rotate our tires, swapping out the front and back tires to the tune of around fifteen to twenty-five dollars. The easiest way to remember to rotate you tires is to get them done every other oil change. You should rotate your tires at least once a year.

3. Wheels in Need of Alignment. Steering and suspension parts wear over time and get bent out of place from driver abuse. This problem can lead to uneven wear on your tires, requiring both a realignment and a tire replacement or two.

4. Unbalanced Tires. Every tire has slight weight imbalances that alter its rotational path. If tires are or become unbalanced, you will notice vibrations or shaking coming from the steering wheel and your seat when driving at speeds over 40 miles per hour. Anytime a tire is removed from the wheel, whether for replacement or for repair, it must be rebalanced by your mechanic after it is replaced.

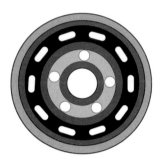

steel wheel

alloy wheel

lug nut

Common Wheel Problems and Fixes

If you forgot all about the wheels those tires are attached to, you're not alone. Since they're not in contact with the ground, wheels get a lot less action than tires do. Unlike tires, they don't require regular maintenance, but every once in a while they may still need a little TLC.

Made of steel or alloy (short for aluminum alloy), each wheel is attached by four to six lug nuts to the wheel bearing, a suspension part that causes the wheel to spin. Also attached to the wheel bearing are the disc or drum brakes. Once the tire is mounted to the wheel, the whole operation (including the brake disc) spins together as the car moves forward or backward. Alloy rims are nice and shiny and don't corrode over time. Steel rims corrode and often wind up looking rusty—which is why they're covered with plastic hubcaps that make the wheel look nice and shiny.

The tire takes most of the beating, but hitting curbs or going over potholes can visibly bend the metal wheel out of shape, which can cause a tire to leak air. When this occurs, you'll need to either have a mechanic bang out the dent or purchase a replacement wheel. Wheels come new or used; since they're just hunks of metal, go for used and save some money. Or knock yourself out with the rims of your dreams. No judgment!

Wheel Alignment Issues

The road of life may sometimes be bumpy. But when it comes to our cars, bumpy, pothole-ridden, and uneven roads can mean death to our tires and our steering and suspension systems. Anyone who has driven on poorly maintained streets knows the pain.

When all four wheels are traveling on an even plane, tire life and fuel economy are maximized and vehicle handling is steady and predictable. In order to ensure that all four tires remain on the ground in any type of road condition, the steering and suspension systems underneath your car are bolted together and set to certain angles when the car is brand-new. But over time, those angles will change slightly, making the car hard to steer and rapidly accelerating tire wear.

This happens with normal wear and tear, but also with damage to the steering and suspension systems. Running over potholes, large bumps, high curbs, and other hazards of the road can knock the steering and suspension components out of place. Once the angles are changed, tire wear happens extremely fast, and steering and suspension parts will start to wear faster as well.

A wheel alignment is the fix that returns the steering and suspension components to their original angles and placements. Your PCT should check both the front and rear wheels, though almost all alignments are needed on the front wheels only. An alignment is sometimes also needed after steering and suspension parts are replaced. Your PCT will let you know.

Signs Your Car Needs a Wheel Alignment

- You feel the car frequently pull, wander, or drift to one side of the road or the other and you have to correct course to continue to drive straight. (A pull to the right or left that occurs during braking is a sign of a brake issue. If you feel the pull while in motion, it's the alignment.)

- You feel a vibration or shimmy while driving, especially at highway speeds.

- The tires show uneven wear (see infographic on page 195). Do not place new tires on a car and then skip the alignment. The tires will wear out extremely fast (maybe in a matter of months).

Wheel and Tire Maintenance and Repairs

Rotating Tires. Rotate your tires every other oil change or at least once a year. Average cost: $15–$25.

Aligning Wheels. Most alignments are clean and painless for PCTs, so they cost less than $100 and can be done in less than forty-five minutes.

Fixing a Bent Wheel. A mechanic can bang out a dent, but a wheel may need replacing if it is bent out of round. Average cost: $100 or less for a used wheel, $200 or less for a new wheel.

Patching a Small Leak. Your PCT may be able to repair a small hole or tear in your tire by inserting a plug, patching the area from the inside of the tire, or using a plug-patch combo. Average cost: $25.

Replacing a Tire. When their tread is worn down, tires need to be replaced. Ideally, we want this wear to happen evenly so that the tire can last 50,000 to 60,000 miles. And on page 194, I'll teach you how to check your tire tread using only a lucky penny. Tires with large punctures, long straight cuts, irregular gashes, or punctures in the shoulder of the sidewall cannot be repaired—they must be replaced. New tires should be the same size as your old ones, so if you're heading to the store yourself, snap a pic of the tire's sidewall, where identifying information is printed, so you have it on hand. It is best practice to match tire brands, too. Average cost of labor and replacement tires: $150 or less per tire for smaller cars, $200 or less per tire for large cars.

TPMS Battery Outage

The tire pressure monitoring system, which lets you know when one of your tires is in need of a puff of air, doesn't itself need much special care. But the battery-operated sensors attached to your tires will give out and need replacing every seven to ten years. The TPMS light will flash instead of illuminating steadily on the dashboard to indicate that the sensor is broken.

Common Auto Airhead Mistakes: Tires

I'm not ashamed to admit that I've personally made four out of these five mistakes. But I expect more from you, ♪#shecanics.

- Ignoring the low tire pressure dashboard light.

- Not rotating tires.

- Not checking the spare tire for air pressure—check pressure yearly. Note: In order to make up for its smaller size, the spare's recommended psi is higher than that of a regular full-size tire.

- Driving over 50 miles an hour on a spare.

- Filling up tires without measuring pressure before and after (see page 191).

- Not having caps on your tire valve stems. Moisture and dirt can enter the tire through the valve stem and cause corrosion at the wheel.

Signs of a Tire or Wheel Issue

Blisters, wobbly heels, slippery soles . . . Your shoes give you feedback when they're getting worn down, and the same goes for your tires and wheels. Look, listen, and feel for the following signs of a tire or wheel issue.

PROBLEM: Vibration in seat or steering wheel

CAUSE: Tires need balancing or lug nuts are loose. The second possibility is dangerous and needs to be addressed ASAP! See step number 8 on page 206 for instructions on tightening your lug nuts yourself.

PROBLEM: Pull or drift of car to one side when driving straight

CAUSE: Steering and/or suspension components are incorrectly angled, and a wheel alignment is needed.

PROBLEM: Correcting the steering wheel to drive straight

CAUSE: Steering and/or suspension components are incorrectly angled, and a wheel alignment is needed.

PROBLEM: Sliding when braking in wet road conditions

CAUSE: Tire tread is low. Tires need to be replaced.

PROBLEM: Leak

CAUSE: Tire has a puncture and may need a patch plug, a valve stem replacement, a remounting, or a replacement.

Your Wheels, Your $$$: Don't Buy Used Tires

While you can generally buy used wheels without a problem, I wouldn't take the risk with tires. Tires are tied with brakes as your car's most important safety features, and you can't stop a car without two functioning pairs.

Used tires, commonly available at independent shops, can sit around for a while. And just like rubber bands, they can crack and lose their plasticity over time from heat and sun. If you have a really trusted PCT, then you might be okay. Just don't play around in this area if you don't know how to pick a good, safe tire.

Special Tires and Fancy Air

There are lots of technical-sounding words in the world of tires. My focus is on getting you to take care of your tires, but here are few distinctions you should understand. Trust me, your wallet will thank you.

All-Wheel-Drive Transmissions. Most AWD vehicles must be equipped with tires that have the same tread depth all around. What does that mean for your wallet? That if your tires have acquired a half-worn tread over 25,000 miles of use, and a single tire requires a replacement due to a flat, blowout, or leak, *all* of the tires must be replaced. You generally can't do a single tire replacement on an AWD vehicle, because driving with one tire whose tread is thicker than the other three can cause expensive transmission damage. Skip AWD vehicles if you don't live somewhere with snowy winters, lots of hills, or dirt roads.

All-Season Tires. Also known as mud-and-snow tires and appropriate for year-round use, these tires are designed to provide traction in light snow or mucky mud conditions.

Snow Tires. Designed with extra tread and made of a rubber compound that remains pliable at very low temperatures, snow tires should not be used all year—the rubber wears out faster during hot summer months and may not perform as well on wet roads.

Run-Flat Tires. Run-flat tires look like conventional tires, but they're designed to be able to function for a little while without any air in them—meaning they won't deflate immediately after a blowout or a large leak. Sounds great, right? But as you probably guessed, there's a catch. They run on empty for only a limited distance, about 50 miles. After which there's an even bigger catch. Run-flat tires are *really* expensive—two to three times the price of a conventional tire. (I once dealt with a car whose run-flat tires were going to cost four hundred bucks each, plus labor, to replace.) Some auto manufacturers use run-flat tires as their defaults, to save on space and weight by eliminating the spare. Know what you're getting, because it may cost you later.

Directional Tires. Designed to optimize tire performance when your car is traveling forward, directional tires look exactly like regular tires but with a tread pattern in the shape of a V. An arrow on the tires' sidewall designates which way is forward, but your PCT should know how to properly mount and rotate these tires.

Low-Profile Tires. The tire of choice for speed lovers, fans of the *Fast and Furious* franchise, and daredevils everywhere, low-profile tires have less sidewall than conventional tires do, giving drivers great control when going around curves at higher speeds. But less tire means less air, and a rougher ride over bumps and potholes. Sports cars with low-profile tires really aren't meant for city driving or intended to be driven every day—a friend of mine who regularly drove his Mustang through Philly traffic was catching a blowout almost every two weeks. And replacing low-profile tires is very expensive. Know what you are getting yourself into, speed demons!

Nitrogen Air. Some shops carry 100 percent compressed nitrogen, and they recommend using it over regular compressed air to fill your tires. They're right. Pure nitrogen is better for your tires, mainly because the oxygen in regular compressed air seeps out through your tire walls over time. The tire filler of choice for race car drivers, nitrogen is more expensive than regular air, which costs little to nothing. Nitrogen shouldn't be mixed with regular air, so if you're going that route, you'll need to be consistent. (When mechanics fill tires with nitrogen air, they'll place green caps on your tire valves to let you know.) Since only some shops offer nitrogen, I'd advise skipping it—unless you really are planning to race that hot rod.

DIY #6: How to Check Air Pressure and Tire Tread

We know how important proper tire pressure is for the life of our tires. But checking tire tread can also help clue us in to problems and potential issues with steering and suspension parts, and tire maintenance should actually be the most frequent of all maintenance tasks. We should be regularly checking our tires for problems, wear, and proper pressure.

Checking Tire Pressure

The proper or operating tire air pressure for most vehicles is 33 psi, but that will vary depending on make and model. Check the air pressure in all your tires every time your tire pressure light comes on and add or remove air as necessary. If a tire pressure gauge didn't come with your car, you can purchase one at a parts store for $10.

When to Check Tire Pressure

- Before going on a road trip longer than two hours
- Monthly if you don't have TPMS
  (required in cars manufactured in 2008 and newer)
- When the tire pressure light illuminates on the dash

Tools

Tire pressure gauge

Gloves (optional)

Air expands as it heats, so checking air pressure when the car is hot will give you a higher reading. For this reason, you should wait until the car is cold (two hours after driving) before measuring the tire pressure if the car has been driven for more than 2 miles.

Unless your dashboard identifies which tire has the low-pressure issue, you'll want to measure all four tires.

1. Kneel to remove the cap from your tire's valve stem. (The setup will look familiar if you've ever taken care of a bicycle.)

2. Make sure the sliding scale at the end of your tire pressure gauge is pushed all the way in. Push the head of the gauge firmly onto the head of the tire valve stem.

3. Once the gauge is in place, you should hear a quick *psst* of air as the gauge's sliding scale edges out. The farther out it edges, the more air pressure there is in the tire. Read the scale to

see the exact pressure. You want the number to match the psi listed on your driver's-side door (see page 21). If air pressure is too low, get some air in those tires ASAP; if air pressure is too high, you'll want to remove some air by detaching the gauge from the tire valve stem for about ten seconds or so.

TIP: *If you hear a long* psssssst *of air coming out instead of a short burst when you place the head of the gauge on the valve stem, you are letting air out of the tire and won't be getting a proper air pressure reading. Readjust the gauge, making sure it fits squarely onto the tire valve stem.*

How to Add Air to Your Tires

The step-by-step for adding air to your tires will vary depending on the particular machine, but it will also involve a tire pressure gauge, attached by a hose to a compressed air machine. Remove the cap from your tire valve stem, then place the gauge on the valve stem as if you were checking the air pressure. Turn the compressed air on—it will make noise while it's working. Make sure the gauge is snugly fastened onto your valve stem, and monitor the amount of air going into the tire to avoid adding too much. Some machines allow you to specify your desired psi and will turn off automatically when that pressure is reached. Quickly replace the cap on your tire valve stem when you're done to avoid losing air.

Measuring Tire Tread

When tires are brand-new, their tread is about 10 inches thick. As you drive and apply the brakes, your tread will wear down. At $\frac{2}{32}$ inches thick, the tire becomes unable to provide optimal traction and thus becomes unsafe. Bald tires can cause a car to slide, especially in quick braking situations, and it takes longer for a car with bald tires to stop. Bald tires will need to be replaced as soon as possible. Try to check tread thickness and wear pattern monthly.

Tool

Penny

Wear bars, also called tire-wear indicators, located between the rows of tire treads, give you easy visual indicators of when your tires need to be replaced.

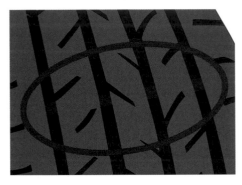

If the wear bar is flush with the tire tread, that means the tread thickness is $2/32$ inches or less, and the tire needs to be replaced.

You can eyeball the wear, but you can also measure the tire tread with a penny.

To do so, turn the penny upside down and place it between two tire treads. If you can see the top of Lincoln's head, your tire's thickness is $2/32$ inches or less and the tire needs to be replaced.

THE SIX DIFFERENT TYPES OF TIRE WEAR

You can easily judge the conditions of your tire tread using nothing but your eyes—uneven wear patterns are very pronounced.

An Underinflated Tire

If the tire tread is more worn on the outsides of the tire than toward the center, the car has been driven for some time with an underinflated tire.

An Overinflated Tire

If the tire tread is more worn toward the center, the car has been driven for some time with the tire overinflated.

Alignment Issues

If the tire tread is more worn on one side than the other, alignment angles are off, and steering need to be realigned.

Alignment Issues (cont.)

If the tire tread appears or feels jagged or feathered, alignment angles are off and steering need to be realigned.

Suspension Issues

Tire treads with bald spots or a scalloped effect are an indication that the car's struts or shocks need to be replaced.

DIY #7:
How to Change
a Tire

Let's be real. Changing a tire is tough, and you're gonna need tools to do it. You're going to get dirty. You might even break a nail. But taking on a new challenge, roughing up your hands, and getting yourself out of a pinch without having to call for help is downright empowering.

There's no shame in a #shecanic paying for roadside assistance and reaping the benefits in times of need. But being able to change a flat is a useful skill. Even if you do have roadside assistance, you never know.

Sometimes even a positive attitude, the right tools, and your best effort won't get the job done. Removing lug nuts with a hand tool can be really difficult, especially if an inexperienced tech bolted your lugs nuts down too tight with a power tool. If you can't change your flat with the tools and techniques listed here, a call to a professional will be in order.

Don't Forget the Spare

How many tires are there on your car? The answer isn't four, or it shouldn't be. Every car should have five tires— four of them attached to the wheels, and a fifth, the spare, tucked beneath the car or in the trunk. Recently automakers have been eliminating the spare tire and tools to decrease the weight of the car and offering spare tire kits as upsells. If your car doesn't come with a spare, I recommend making the investment.

What Causes a Flat Tire

- Puncture of a tire by a sharp object such as a nail, causing a small or large air leak

- Running of a tire against the curb or collision with a car or other object, causing small or large air leaks depending on the extent of the damage

- Excessive wear of tire tread, creating explosive tire failure, or tearing by road debris, resulting in large air leaks

- Failure of or damage to valve stem causing small air leaks

There's no way of anticipating the random, nasty sharp object that takes a bite out of your tire and ruins your day. But you can decrease your chances of a flat by inflating your tires to the proper psi (not too high, not too low), rotating your tires at least once a year, and making sure that your tire tread isn't worn down too far. Those of you who've been reading carefully will remember that this was never much of a Patrice specialty. I wore my tires *down*. And as someone who's always running around like a chicken with her head cut off, I never appreciated having to make an unexpected stop at the gas station just so I could scrounge around for a bunch of coins to put a tiny little puff of air in my tires. I ignored that tire pressure light like it was a call from a life insurance salesman. It's honestly a miracle that I never skidded out in the middle of the highway with a blowout on one of those cross-country trips of mine.

Don't be the ghost of Patrice past. Keep your tires healthy by staying on schedule with those tire rotations and replacements— and making a stop at the gas station when your dashboard tells you that your tires need a refill.

Or, take it up a notch by buying a portable compressor for fifteen to thirty dollars. You'll never have to deal with the annoyance of an unexpected stop at the gas station air machine. And if you do pop a slow leak, a compressor might allow you to temporarily refill the sagging tire and drive yourself (very carefully) to a repair shop—a totally worthwhile investment.

How Long Were You Parked?

If you catch a flat while parked . . . how long were you parked? You most likely have a leak from an object stuck in the tire, the valve stem, or the tire bead. If your car has been parked for more than twenty-four hours, you may have the type of small leak that could be temporarily inflated with a portable compressor, giving you enough air to tide you over on the drive to the closest garage or tire shop. If your car has been parked for less than twenty-four hours, change the tire on the spot—the leak is too large, and you might not make it to the closest garage or tire shop. Small, slow air leaks deflate a tire over the course of a few days; tires with slow leaks can often be repaired and reinflated, unless their tread is worn. Large, fast air leaks can deflate a tire in minutes or seconds. The latter is what you call a blowout, the very worst kind of flat.

Safety First

If you get a flat while driving, make sure to pull off somewhere safe. Changing a tire with your back to traffic can be extremely dangerous for you or for a roadside mechanic. If your flat is on the right side of the car, try to pull over to the right side of the road; if your flat is on the left, pull off to the left.

Get yourself to flat ground if possible, apply your emergency brake, and turn on your hazard lights. Never change a tire on a hill or incline. If you can't reach flat ground, you'll need to get a tow.

If you have an orange cone or triangle warning (see page 282), place it behind the car to make yourself that much more visible.

Tools of the Trade

Think gathering all the tools needed to change a flat means a trip to the auto parts store? Think again—these tools should actually come with your car. They're usually tucked away beneath the carpeted layer of your trunk or strapped underneath the trunk. If you're buying a used car, check to make sure they're all there. Here's what you'll need:

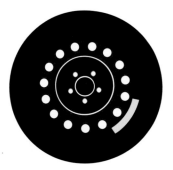

Spare tire or full-size spare—required

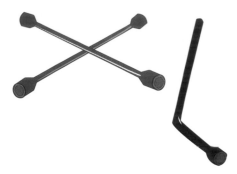

Lug wrench (X-shaped or L-shaped)—required to remove lug nuts from wheel studs

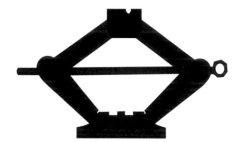

Jack—required to lift the car off the ground

Mat—nice to have for when you are on your hands and knees finding the lift points

Gloves—highly recommended to keep hands clean and free from injury

Pipe—nice to have for extra leverage when removing lug nuts

How to Change a Tire

If you've got the tools and you've got the spare, you're ready to change your tire. I've provided instructions here, but check your owner's manual for details on how to use your particular jack and the locations of your lift points—the spots on your car where you can safely position the jack. Using a jack isn't always intuitive, so if your owner's manual doesn't do it for you, see my "Changing a Tire" video on YouTube for help.

Now put on your gloves and place your mat on the ground next to your flat tire. Time to get dirty!

1. **Find the lift points for the jack.** Place the jack on the car's problem side and get on your hands and knees to locate the lift point closest to the tire you are changing—this is the spot where a jack can be safely positioned. There are four lift points on a car, located several inches behind the front tires and several inches in front of the rear tires (and designated on some cars with little arrows).

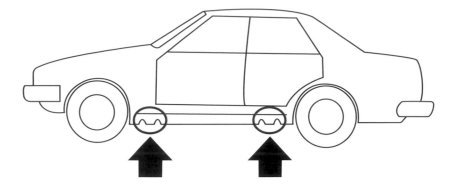

Locate your lift points.

2. Position the jack and prep the tire. Place the jack on flat ground directly beneath the lift point. Start to raise the jack until the top touches the lift point on the car. Jack the car up just enough to get a little weight off the tire. *Do not* jack the car all the way up so that the tire leaves the ground. If you do, when you try to loosen the lug nuts, the tire will spin and prevent you from obtaining traction.

3. Bust a nut. Grab your lug wrench—it's time to bust loose the lug nuts (the parts that secure the tire to the wheel bearing) from the wheel studs.

Make sure the head of your wrench fits tightly around the lug nut and is pushed all the way onto the lug. Remember the toy toddlers would play with, where they had to put the square peg in the square hole and the circular peg in the circular hole? Same philosophy here.

Turn the wrench counterclockwise to loosen the lug nuts.

Now turn the wrench to the left (counterclockwise), exerting as much force as you can on the end of the wrench. Remember: righty tighty, lefty loosey. The trick here is to loosen the lug nuts enough so you will be able to remove them later by hand. Do not remove them from the stud yet.

Loosen all of the lug nuts. The tire will still be on the ground.

Those lug nuts can be stubborn, so this step is likely to be the hardest part. Lug nuts may be rusted on, or they could have been screwed on too tight the last time the tire was removed. Mechanics use a power tool to screw and unscrew lug nuts, and some really drill down onto the wheel stud.

There are a couple of things you can do to loosen your lug nuts if you find that using your own upper body strength is not sufficient: (a) use your foot to step on the wrench,

If needed, use your body weight for leverage.

recruiting your body weight to create some extra force, or (b) slide the pipe from your tool kit over the handle of the wrench. This will lengthen the wrench handle, giving you more mechanical leverage and decreasing the force required to turn the lug.

4. Lift the car. Once the lug nuts are all loose, jack up the car until the flat tire is *just* off the ground and the wheel can spin freely. Now you'll be lifting part of the car off the ground. This will give your arms a serious workout, but you can do it.

5. Remove the tire. Once the flat tire is off the ground, use your hands to completely remove all the lug nuts from the wheel studs. Place the lug nuts aside. Pull the flat tire off the wheel studs and place it aside as well.

6. Put on the spare. Grab the spare and place it on the wheel. Retrieve the lug nuts and use your hands to screw them onto the wheel studs. Remember, righty tighty, lefty loosey. Do not use any tools to tighten the lug nuts yet. You want them to be "hand tight," just holding the tire onto the wheel.

7. Lower the car. Now it's time to lower the car with the jack until the tire just touches the ground. Do not completely lower the weight of the car onto the ground. You want the car in the same position as in step 3, when you were busting the nuts loose. You don't want the entire weight of the car on the spare tire until the lug nuts have been tightened with a wrench.

8. Tighten the lug nuts (see opposite). Take your lug wrench and tighten each lug nut onto its stud, starting at the top right and working in a star pattern. Remember to make sure the head of your wrench fits tightly around the lug nut and is pushed all the way on.

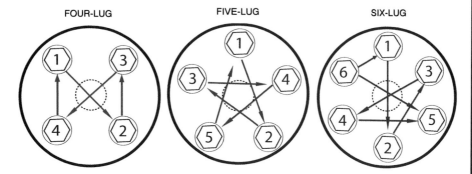

FOUR-LUG   FIVE-LUG   SIX-LUG

Follow the star pattern to evenly bolt tires onto wheel studs and prevent lug nuts from "backing out" or becoming unthreaded and flying off as you drive; the pattern changes depending on the number of lug nuts on your wheels.

Use some muscle when you turn the wrench to the right (clockwise). You can recruit your foot or the pipe to get more leverage on the wrench, but you don't need to jump on it. You do want to use all your might, wrenching down on the lug until the wrench doesn't turn any farther.

9. Remove the jack. Almost there! Now it's time to lower the jack all the way. Put your tools, along with the flat tire, back into the trunk. Take the tire to your mechanic to get it repaired or replaced.

10. The final and most important step? Wipe your brow and stand back and admire your hard work.

Fast Facts About Flat and Spare Tires

Most of us pay little attention to that spare tire in the back, but just like the rest of your car, it sometimes requires a little TLC. Here's a bit more about how to care for the most valuable player on your bench.

Keep your spare inflated. You can't change a flat tire with a flat spare, and tires lose air over time even if they aren't being used. So make sure you or your PCT checks the tire pressure on your spare at least once a year.

Know your size. A full-size spare, often seen in SUVs and trucks, is not limited in its functionality. But a spare tire, often called a space saver or a donut, is deliberately sized down to save on space and weight. For this reason, a spare is meant to be used only temporarily. Driving around on a small

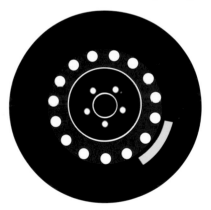

spare tire for long periods of time is a major no-no that can result in damage to suspension parts and other components of your car. Do not drive over speeds of 50 miles an hour on a spare (i.e., stay away from highways), and avoid driving in adverse weather conditions.

A quick fix for small leaks. For flat tires with small leaks, emergency aerosol sealants and inflators like Fix-A-Flat can be used as temporary solutions that will allow you to get to a mechanic. You may need to add air before sealing the leak, so a portable compressor will come in handy. These products

Sealants and inflators may prevent the tire pressure light from working properly.

will not work on a leak that is too large or on a completely flat tire. They should be used only when absolutely necessary, as they may cause damage to the expensive tire pressure monitoring sensors present on cars manufactured from 2008 on; these are the sensors responsible for illuminating that handy low tire pressure light on your dashboard, so you don't want to mess with them.

Steering: Navigating Your Chariot

With nothing but the slightest nudge of the wheel, you glide your 4,000-pound baby into the tightest parking spots and around the gnarliest turns. It's time to talk steering, the system that allows you to navigate winding mountain roads or dodge through rush-hour traffic. The steering process involves force, fluid, and all the metal rods and links that connect the steering wheel to the wheels on your car. But if one of the links in that chain is compromised, all that Fahrvergnügen can go flying right out the window.

Without power steering, even the combined force of two adult humans cannot steer a car. Just as with your car's braking system, you've got hydraulics and a Super Mario Bros. power boost to thank for the fact that you don't need a superhero's biceps to exert total control.

Anatomy of Your Steering System

The process of steering a car starts with a casual turn of your hand on the wheel, command central for navigation. The wheel is connected to a series of gears and parts that, when given a boost from the power steering system, manipulates the wheels to the right or left, enabling the car to turn.

Here's a breakdown of the parts involved. (See the illustration on page 212 to get a sense of how it all comes together.)

Steering Wheel. Turns the car left or right. Connects to the steering column and ultimately to the wheels of the car.

Steering Column. A shaft connecting the steering wheel to the gears inside the steering rack.

Steering Rack. A long transverse bar that moves from side to side when the gears it contains are rotated by the steering column.

Steering Linkage. Several arms, rods, or links that connect the steering rack to the front wheels of the car. The ones you are most likely to hear about are the inner tie rods, outer tie rods, and Pitman arm.

Power Steering System. The Super Mario Bros. boost or assist that allows the driver to turn the steering wheel. Its components include the reservoir that holds the power steering fluid, the pump and hoses that move the fluid around, and the drive or serpentine belt and pulley, which trigger the pump. Your power steering system is fairly easy and inexpensive to maintain, so there are no excuses when it comes to giving a little bit of that scheduled TLC (see Maintenance and Repairs chart).

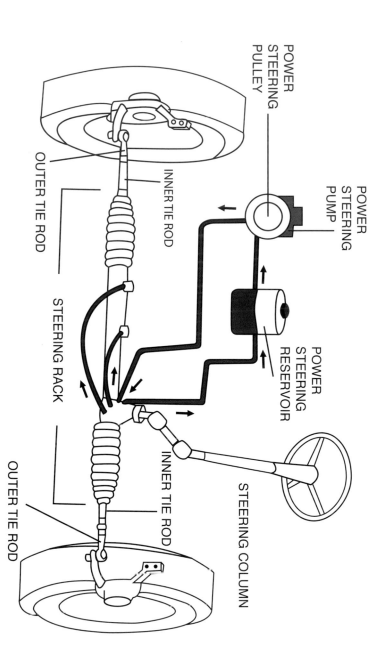

POWER STEERING PULLEY

POWER STEERING PUMP

POWER STEERING RESERVOIR

OUTER TIE ROD

INNER TIE ROD

STEERING RACK

OUTER TIE ROD

INNER TIE ROD

STEERING COLUMN

A series of racks, links, arms, and rods connect your steering wheel to your tires, and a hydraulic boost from your power steering system provides the muscle to get the job done.

What's That Grinding Noise?

While loud grinding noises are indications of a probable steering issue, it's normal to hear *some* grinding or whining when your steering wheel is turned all the way to the left or to the right, as in parallel parking. There's a lot of pressure and force being applied throughout the steering rack during a parallel parking maneuver, and some amount of noise is a natural result. If you hear loud grinding noises regularly while driving and turning, check your power steering fluid (see page 172).

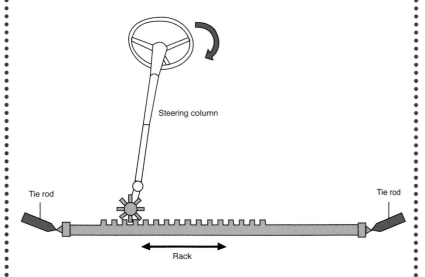

An internal view of the steering rack (pictured opposite) reveals the gears at the center of the operation.

STEERING MAINTENANCE AND REPAIRS

PART	ISSUE	FIX	TIMING	COST
Power Steering Fluid	Over time, power steering fluid will pick up water and chemically break down, causing it to evaporate or boil off at a lower temperature. This decreases the fluid level in your reservoir. Without enough fluid in your power steering system, you won't be able to turn the steering wheel, and you'll eventually cause damage to the steering rack	Fluid flush	Every three to five years	$200 or less
Power Steering Pump	Low fluid can cause a pump to wear out, but pumps also wear over time	Replace	When fluid leaks or pump fails	$500 and up
Steering Rack	Steering racks can spring a leak, lowering your supply of power steering fluid. Their gears can also become worn or bound up. If a rack is leaking at the seals, power steering fluid will be low, and you may hear loud grinding or whining noises or encounter lots of resistance when turning the steering wheel. If the gears are worn, the wheel will feel very loose	Generally, replacement	When fluid leaks or rack fails	Rack jobs involve many hours of labor, and unfortunately tend to require pump and hose replacements as well; $750 and up

PART	ISSUE	FIX	TIMING	COST
Steering Linkage	Potholes and high curbs are kryptonite to the steering linkage, which can bend or break and wear over time, particularly at the inner or outer tie-rod ends. When it's time to replace elements of the steering linkage, you'll hear knocks or loud bumps when turning or going over potholes	Replace	Normally not until at least 60,000 to 70,000 miles	Mechanics recommend replacing these in pairs. If one side is going bad, the other side will fail soon after. An alignment is often needed after steering linkage is replaced; $150–$500 per side
Power Steering Hoses	Leak. There is a high-pressure power steering hose and a low-pressure power steering hose; both will tend to leak from use over time	Replace	When hoses leak or fail	$350 and up

Signs of a Power Steering Issue

Got a steering wheel that locks up, feels hard to turn, or feels extremely loose? These are obvious signs of a steering issue. But if you hear loud grinding, bumping, whining, or knocking noises while turning the wheel, you likely have a steering issue as well.

Whining noises in the steering rack can result from low or dirty power steering fluid. That might simply mean you're in need of a fluid flush (see page 71), but such noises could also be signs of a leak in the system. Power steering failures aren't all that common, but if they're ignored, they can lead to safety issues and faster wear of the overall steering system.

Know that power steering problems tend to be expensive, because often multiple parts need to be replaced. Replacing a power steering rack sometimes requires replacement of the power steering pressure hoses and the pump, costing close to $2,000.

Suspension: Giving You That Smooth Ride

Keeping the wheels connected to the frame and all four tires on the road, the suspension system is every driver's best friend. Without it, the ride would be rough, your tires would wear out extremely fast, and your car would be bouncing off the ground anytime you hit a bump. Imagine a bouncing ball hitting a rock and pinging off in a random direction. That's how our cars would behave without the suspension system. Without suspension, there is no control.

The suspension system doesn't require any maintenance. Parts will fail over time, or due to physical damage. (Running over curbs, hitting potholes, getting caught in minor crashes, or driving over road hazards can all cause significant damage.) But unless you drive a truck with greasable bearings, you don't need to do anything to maintain this part of the car if everything is running smoothly. And given normal wear and tear, suspension system parts don't start failing until you've clocked around 80,000 miles.

Anatomy of the Suspension System

The suspension system is symmetrical, with many of its parts coming in pairs. What that means as far as maintenance is that if the right front wheel has a wheel bearing that's going bad or has failed, the left front wheel bearing is picking up the slack and being worked harder. It will likely fail soon as well, which is why mechanics often recommend replacing suspension parts such as struts, shock absorbers, ball joints, bushings, and wheel bearings in pairs. Here are the main components of the suspension system and where they fit into the picture.

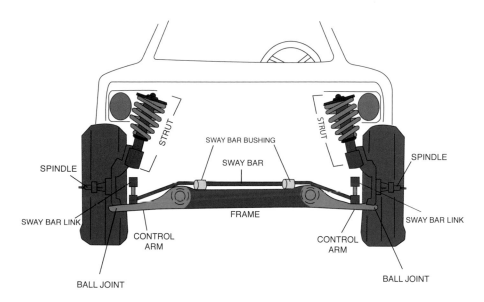

Springs, Struts. Absorb shock and vibrations from driving on bumpy roads. Will fail from use over time.

Rods, Bars, and Links. Help with stability of the car while turning. Will fail from use over time.

Bushings. Rubber and plastic pieces that absorb shock and vibration. Will fail over time, cracking and becoming less pliable.

Wheel Bearings or Hub Bearings. Expensive components that allow the wheels to rotate. Wheel bearings support the weight of the vehicle.

Steering Knuckles, Ball Joints, and Control Arms. All the previously listed suspension parts are connected to the steering knuckle (aka spindle) and control arms through ball joints. Steering knuckles don't normally exhibit issues unless they suffer physical damage, but ball joints will fail over time; often the entire control arm will need to be replaced instead of just the ball joint.

Smart Suspension Systems

Some luxury cars feature electronic suspensions with controls, sensors, and switches that allow drivers to tweak suspension in response to different road conditions. A driver may want to tighten suspension when going around corners at high speed or during quick acceleration or braking. While cruising, you would opt for a softer ride.

In standard vehicles, the only suspension system sensor is the wheel speed sensor attached to your wheel bearings. Flip back to page 162 for more on how this sensor helps manage your ABS system.

Signs of a Suspension Issue

Failed or failing suspension parts will make *a lot* of noise. Listen for creaks, whines, bumps, thumps, humming, and thuds coming from your car's wheels as you drive. The car may also pull or wander left or right or vibrate while you drive. Unevenly worn tires can also be signs of a suspension issue. Listen carefully to see whether sounds are coming from the right or left side of the car—this is helpful information for your PCT.

Common Auto Airhead Mistake: Suspension

There's only one thing you can do wrong here: Turning up the radio and continuing to drive your car while it is making unusual noises. You could be doing expensive damage to your suspension system, so take your car in to your PCT for a diagnosis.

Heating and Air-Conditioning: Keeping It Cozy

Any *♪#shecanic* who's gotten work done on her climate control system knows that repairs in this area can get seriously expensive. Neither heating nor air-conditioning is required to run the car, but could we really live without them? In the middle of summer, as heat gets trapped inside via a phenomenon called the greenhouse effect, the internal temperature of a parked car can reach levels that are actually life-threatening. And who'd be crazy enough to try driving around without heat on a 30-degree day?

Climate control is definitely an example of engineering at its best—but when the price tag for those repairs comes in, the system can seem more like an example of luxury at its worst. Like any other system in our cars, the more technology attached (electronic climate control, heated seating), the more potential points of failure. So the same rule of thumb applies as in all areas of vehicular financing: Don't buy more climate control than you can afford to maintain. Even without bells and whistles, AC repairs are very expensive because, like power steering failures, they often involve several parts at once.

Ice, Ice, Baby

Have you ever used a can of compressed air to clean computer components? The can gets ice cold when you squeeze or pump the compressed air out of the small nozzle. This temperature drop is due to the rapid expansion of compressed air, and the same thing happens inside your car's air-conditioning system: Liquid Freon is squeezed through a small valve, cooling down the car when it expands.

Here are the major components of the system that keeps you cool as a cucumber.

Air. Outside ambient air.

Freon. Chemical refrigerant pumped through the AC system by a compressor.

Compressor. Pump that circulates Freon throughout the AC system. Located under the hood and attached to the engine crankshaft by a pulley and belt.

Accumulator. Reservoir where liquid Freon is stored and any foreign particles or matter are trapped before they can clog the expansion valve or orifice tube.

Expansion Valve or Orifice Tube. Part located under the hood through which Freon is pumped into the evaporator.

Evaporator. The container through which liquid Freon passes as it's being converted into a hot vaporized gas. Hot outside air is blown past the ice-cold evaporator to cool down before being circulated into the car. Located in the dashboard, next

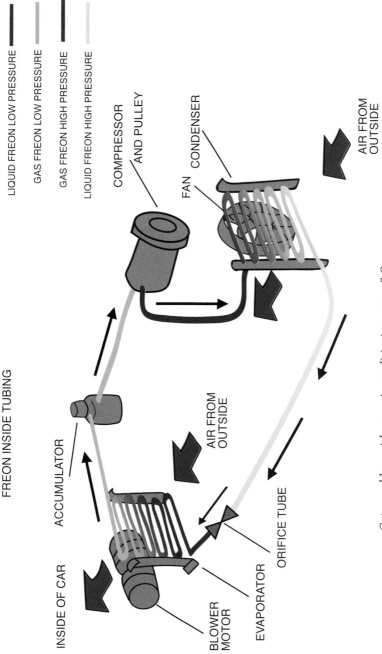

LIQUID FREON LOW PRESSURE

GAS FREON LOW PRESSURE

GAS FREON HIGH PRESSURE

LIQUID FREON HIGH PRESSURE

COMPRESSOR AND PULLEY

FAN CONDENSER

AIR FROM OUTSIDE

FREON INSIDE TUBING

ACCUMULATOR

AIR FROM OUTSIDE

INSIDE OF CAR

BLOWER MOTOR

EVAPORATOR

ORIFICE TUBE

Got a problem with your air-conditioning system? One or more of the pictured parts will probably need to be replaced.

to the heater core and blower motor, the evaporator also works as a dehumidifier, as moisture from the hot air collects on the outside of the cold evaporator.

Condenser. Sits in front of the radiator, converting vaporized Freon coming from the compressor back into a liquid. A fan blows air past the condenser to cool it down.

Belt and Pulley. The serpentine or drive belt and an AC compressor pulley, which connect to the engine's crankshaft to power the AC compressor.

AC Lines. Aluminum tubing and rubber hoses that connect all the components of the AC system.

Frost and Fog

The defrost button and setting comes to the rescue when a windshield is fogged up with hot, moist air or frosted over in cold weather. But if your car has automatic heating and AC controls, the AC will automatically come on when you turn on the defrost; on cars without automatic controls, you'll want to turn on the AC manually. The reason why? The AC acts as a dehumidifier, removing moisture from the exterior air before it is blown onto your windshield.

The heating and AC system contains three controls: the temperature dial or button, the fan speed dial, and the dial or switch button that turns on the AC. Here's how you should set them for optimal defrosting or defogging:

- Set airflow controls to defrost. If it doesn't come on automatically, turn AC on.

- Set temperature controls as desired—cool in the summer, warm in the winter.

- To speed up defrosting or defogging, set your fan speed to high.

If turning on the AC when it's cold out sounds weird, worry not. As long as your temperature controls are set to hot, hot air will still blow out into your car. Remember, heat and AC are two different systems that share only an air delivery component. When the AC is on but the temperature control is set to hot, air will blow past the AC first to shed moisture, than past the heater core to warm up.

COOLANT BOTTLE RESERVOIR

THERMOSTAT

AIR FROM
OUTSIDE

RADIATOR CAP

FAN

RADIATOR

WATER/COOLANT PUMP

ENGINE

The best part about your car's heating system?
It runs on heat generated by the hardworking engine.

HEATER CORE

BLOWER
MOTOR

INSIDE OF CAR

Hot Fire

Most people don't know that your automobile's heating system runs on recycled, redirected engine heat. When the heater is on, hot coolant is redirected through a small radiator on its way out of the engine. Air blown over the radiator picks up the coolant's ambient heat, and the inside of the car gets nice and toasty.

Since the heating system uses the engine's cooling system to procure heat, most of its components, with the exception of the heater core and valves, are already contained within the engine coolant system.

> **Heater Core.** A small radiator located under the dash, the heater core provides heat to passengers as needed. When the heat is off, hot coolant leaves the engine and goes straight to the thermostat and radiator. When you turn on the heat via your dash heater control, a valve opens, sending coolant from the engine into the heater core before it goes on to the thermostat. As hot coolant flows through and heats the heater core, air passes across the heater core and picks up heat before it is redirected into the car.

Parts Shared by the AC and Heating Systems

> **Blower Motor.** Fan that blows outside air across the cold evaporator or hot heater core and into the car.

> **Cabin Air Filter.** Filters the outside air before it reaches your lungs.

Smart Controls

Cars with automatic controls are loaded up with sensors that monitor and regulate internal and external temperatures. But even cars with basic systems use computerized functions to monitor climate control. If Freon gets too cold, the evaporator could freeze into a block of ice—so a sensor monitors the coolant temperature and shuts off the AC compressor if things are getting too icy.

Puddles, Dampness, and Invisible Leaks

"Help, there's something leaking under my car!" That's a panicky email or text I've gotten pretty used to seeing. My first question is "What color is it?" If the answer is "clear, like water," I smile and congratulate the sender.

In the process of helping circulate ice-cold air into your car, the evaporator itself gets ice-cold. Moisture from the hot air that blows across the cold evaporator collects and condenses on the outside of the evaporator. This condensed moisture then tends to drip onto the ground—kind of like morning dew on the grass. Nothing to get worked up about, just a little dew. In fact, this condensation is a sign that your AC is working properly. The water will almost always appear under the passenger side of the car, where the evaporator in the AC system is located.

If your the passenger side carpet is getting wet, that's another issue. The evaporator water drip tube that directs the evaporator's condensation to the ground has gotten clogged with dirt, leaves, or mud, and moisture is leaking from the evaporator housing into the interior of the car.

If you have a Freon leak, on the other hand, you won't be able to see it—because at room temperature, Freon is a gas, not a liquid. As soon as Freon leaks out of your AC system, it evaporates. To detect a suspected leak, mechanics feed a special dye into the AC system.

AC SYSTEM MAINTENANCE AND REPAIRS

PART	ISSUE	FIX	TIMING	COST
Evaporator	Can leak from age and use over time, or become clogged by particles in the Freon	Replace	Could fail at any time but should last at least 60,000 miles	Replacing this part is very expensive, because just getting to the evaporator (located under the dash in most cars) is labor-intensive. Look to spend at least $750. Since the evaporator and heater core are right next to each other, PCTs recommend replacing both simultaneously.
Condenser	Can leak from age and use over time, or become clogged by particles in the Freon; may also leak as a result of damage caused by rocks and debris	Replace	Could fail at any time but should last at least 60,000 miles	At least $300

PART	ISSUE	FIX	TIMING	COST
Compressor	The compressor and/or compressor clutch will fail from use over time, or due to exposure to moisture or particles in the Freon	Replace	Could fail at any time but should last at least 60,000 miles	This is an expensive part, and the job will likely cost $500 and up
Expansion Valve or Orifice Tube	When this part becomes clogged, the flow of Freon is blocked, causing warm air to blow into the car when the AC is turned on	Replace	Could fail at any time but should last at least 60,000 miles	Less than $500
AC Lines and Hoses	These parts can fail at connections, leaking refrigerant	Replace	Could fail at any time but should last at least 60,000 miles	Varies

HEATING SYSTEM

PART	ISSUE	FIX	TIMING	COST
Heater Hose	Hoses will wear, crack, and fail over time, or from being exposed to excessive heat	Replace	Could fail at any time but should last at least 60,000 miles	Hoses are inexpensive parts, but getting to them can be difficult; replace heater hoses when you replace the heater core

PART	ISSUE	FIX	TIMING	COST
Heater Core	The heater core can leak coolant from age and use or become clogged by particles in the coolant	Replace. Sometimes mechanics turn off the heater control valve, allowing coolant to bypass the heater core. This sacrifices climate control but doesn't compromise engine function	Could fail at any time but should last at least 60,000 miles	Replacing this part is very expensive because just getting to the heater core (located under the dash in most cars) is labor-intensive. Look to spend at least $750 to replace. Replace simultaneously with evaporator (see page 229) and you will pay only the additional cost of the evaporator

SHARED PARTS

PART	ISSUE	FIX	TIMING	COST
Cabin Air Filter	Becomes clogged with dust and hair	Replace	Per your owner's manual, or at least once a year if you have kids or pets in the car	Normally less than $40
Blower Motor	Blower motors can quit on you whenever they feel like it	Replace. If the issue is limited to the blower motor resistor, which controls motor speed and airflow, only the resistor will need replacing	Could fail at any time but should last at least 60,000 miles	For motor, varies greatly, from $100 to $750, depending on how easy the part is to access. For resistor only, less than $250

PART	ISSUE	FIX	TIMING	COST
Fan	The electrical fan turned on by the alternator can fail from use over time, or from physical damage caused by rocks or debris being kicked up underneath the car; signs of failure include no or intermittent heat or AC	Replace	Could fail at any time but should last at least 60,000 miles	Less than $500

Signs of an AC or Heat Issue

PROBLEM: Lukewarm air when you want AC

POSSIBLE CAUSES:

- Block in the system. Usually dirt from corrosion or rusting of metal parts, causing lines to be blocked.

- Low coolant level. Freon has leaked (evaporating into thin air) and isn't around to do its job.

- AC compressor malfunction. Check compressor, serpentine or drive belt, and compressor pulley.

- Fan not working. May need replacing.

PROBLEM: Lukewarm or cold air when you want heat

POSSIBLE CAUSES:

- Block in the heater core. Usually dirt from corrosion or rusting of the engine and other metal parts, causing lines to be blocked.

- Low coolant level. Another reason to stay on top of your coolant.

- Thermostat valve stuck open. May need replacing.

- Fan not working. May need replacing.

PROBLEM: Water on the front passenger-side carpet

POSSIBLE CAUSE:

- Clogged evaporator water drip tube

PROBLEM: No or low airflow

POSSIBLE CAUSES:

- Blower motor or blower motor resistor needs replacing

- Cabin air filter needs replacing

PROBLEM: No change in airflow when you try to increase fan speed, or only the highest speed works

POSSIBLE CAUSE:

- Blower motor or blower motor resistor needs replacing

PROBLEM: Rattling noises when heat or AC is on

POSSIBLE CAUSE:

- Blower motor needs replacing

Gas: The Joys and Pains

There are just a few things I despise in life: traffic, 7:00 A.M. meetings, mosquitoes. Oh, and pumping gas. When you cut things down to the wire like I do, an unexpected five minutes at the gas pump can really put a wrinkle in your day.

Gas is a necessary evil in the lives of many, but fortunately, there are a few things we can all do to reduce the frequency of our trips to the gas station, save money, and help decrease pollution.

Regular, Midgrade, and Premium: What's the Diff?

Let's start with a fundamental choice, a decision many of us make in a split second at the pump: what kind of gas to use in our cars. The octane ratings for "regular"-grade fuel range from 85 to 87, with "midgrade" clocking in at 88 to 90 and "premium" at 91 and above. The ratings correspond to the fuel's blend and additives, which determine the temperature at which the fuel is burned. Typically, you get a choice between 87, 89, and 93.

Contrary to popular belief, burning premium fuel doesn't translate into extra energy in your car. Gasoline engines are designed to burn fuel at certain temperatures, so putting premium fuel in an engine designed to burn regular gas is just a waste of your money. Higher-octane premium fuels allow more advanced engine designs to pull additional power from each gallon of gasoline. These  fuels are used in high-performance gasoline engines, such as those found in a Mercedes or BMW.

Using fuel with lower octane than the one your engine calls for *will* affect power and performance and wear out your spark plugs faster. You may hear a pinging in the engine or see the check-engine light come on. The higher-octane gas will result in a nicer ride in luxury vehicles designed for performance and power. You may decrease engine performance and eventually create problems if you do this regularly. But you will not do significant damage to your engine by occasionally using regular if your owner's manual calls for premium. Think of it this way: If you can't afford premium gas, you can't afford a luxury car.

How can you find out what kind of gas to use? Check your owner's manual or the inside of the car's fuel door.

What About Diesel?

Used in certain cars and large trucks, diesel fuel is generally more expensive than gasoline—but it is also more efficient. Diesel can be used only by diesel engines, which spontaneously combust the gas (heating and compressing it to the point where it explodes on its own, without the aid of a spark).

Gas pumps are designed to make it very difficult or impossible to accidentally use the wrong gas, but *do not* put diesel gasoline in a gas engine. You will damage your fuel system.

Don't Top Off Your Gas Tank!

Whether you're trying to save a penny, avoid the gas station, or nudge the payment to an even $30.00 instead of that pesky $29.53, when you top off your gas tank, you risk causing damage to your vehicle and polluting the environment. In order to leave room for your emissions and fuel systems to operate properly, gas pumps are specifically designed to turn off when fuel reaches a certain level in your tank. Overriding that function is a very bad idea, and there are three reasons why.

1. Your gas tank contains both liquid fuel *and* vapors. Fuel expands, especially when it's hot out. As it

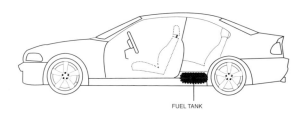

FUEL TANK

expands, vapors are forced out of the fuel tank and into your car's emissions system, where they are collected and stored. Eventually, they are rerouted to the engine, where they are burned along with liquid fuel pumped from the tank. If you top off your tank, liquid fuel will be forced into an emissions system that is designed to admit only fuel vapors. This can damage the emissions system and set off your check-engine light. You'll need to replace damaged parts of the emissions system, most likely the evaporative charcoal canister.

2. Additional gas you try to pump into your tank may be drawn back into the vapor line and fed back into the pump. Whoops. Now you just paid for gas that was returned to the station. It's pennies, but still.

3. Any time you top off your tank, you increase the likelihood of spilling gas on the ground and releasing gas vapors into the air, both of which are very bad for the environment.

The moral of the story? Top off your coffee, not your gas tank.

No Living on E

I'm a last-minute girl. Planning, cleaning, cooking for a party, catching a plane, driving to work. You name it. Take my habit of waiting until my gas tank was on E . . . and then waiting a bit longer before getting gas. Hey, I ran out of gas only that one time! Little did I know, my trick for avoiding the gas station had some big ramifications.

Here's why: When you do finally get your rear end to the gas station, that liquid gold flows into a large tank located directly beneath the backseat. A pump propels the fuel to the front of the car, so that it can be injected into the engine. That pump must be working efficiently—and the fuel itself is essential to that process, because it also acts as a lubricant and coolant for the hardworking pump. When you run your tank on empty, the pump has to work a

whole lot harder and may burn out. Now no gas is getting to the engine, and your car won't start. Your procrastinating ways could cost you a tow, along with the price of having a new fuel pump installed. Not a cheap job. To avoid getting into the danger zone, make sure you always have at least a quarter tank's worth of gas.

Running on fumes can damage your fuel pump—stay well out of the red zone to save yourself $$$.

Your Wheels, Your $$$: Ways to Increase Fuel Economy

Want to find out how to lower your gas bill and reduce your trips to the gas station? Follow these tips for fuel economy and optimal vehicular health.

- Keep tires inflated to the proper air pressure. Low tire pressure will cause greater fuel consumption.

- Regularly attend to oil and air filter changes and tune-ups.

- Do not ignore the check-engine light, which comes on when the vehicle is not burning fuel efficiently. Take your car to your PCT to find out why the light is on.

- Remove any extra load. In other words, clean out your ride.

- Don't drive like a New York City cabbie. Hard braking and fast acceleration eat gas.

- Just say no to speed racing. The faster you drive, the more drag on the vehicle, the more work the engine must do, the more gas you burn. Try to keep the rpm (gauge on dashboard) around 2, which stands for 2,000 revolutions per minute. Still pretty darn fast.

Part iii

COMMON ROADSIDE PROBLEMS

(AND A MINI BUYER'S GUIDE)

Buy, Sell, Ditch: How to Avoid a Clunker (or Tell When Your Car Has Become One) and Buy a Car You Can Afford

Remember when you first started driving? The thrill of passing the big test, that first time you pulled out of your parents' driveway and peeled away on your own? I'll never love another car the way I loved my first. But I wish that instead of just grilling me on obscure traffic regulations, the driver's test had given me some inkling of the responsibility involved not just in driving, but in actually owning a car.

Before I went to auto tech school, that responsibility wasn't on my radar at all. When I was ready to purchase a car, I'd head to the dealership, pick a car I liked out of a lineup, test-drive it, and take it home. I didn't think about other factors that might affect me and my wallet. Terms like *horsepower* meant nothing to me, and I had no idea of the difference between a V-6 and a V-8 engine. If the car looked good and felt good to drive, I took it home. Maybe in my next life I'll be reborn as a wheeler and dealer.

In this chapter we're going to talk about buying and selling cars, but I'm not going to give you my top ten negotiation tips or tell you how to finance your rig. Those aren't my areas. What I am going to cover is what all ♩#shecanics must know: understanding the true cost of owning a car. Knowing what you'll really be paying over the car's lifetime will help you purchase the right car, and then know when it's time to end your love affair.

Before You Buy

Having a good relationship with your car starts with choosing the right car. Because the amount of attention and care a car requires can vary a *whole* lot, the decision will have serious ramifications for your wallet. I had no idea what I was getting myself into when I purchased my first brand-new car, and later ran into many repairs I couldn't afford. Cue buyer's remorse, three years after my purchase. I wanted to blame the mechanics, the dealerships, the manufacturer—everyone. But ultimately I hadn't chosen the right car for me. I didn't know how.

Understanding the Costs of Ownership

One thing I say in all my workshops is that every part on a car will fail eventually. Everything on your car that moves can break, wear, rust, malfunction, or lose efficiency. Members of the ♩#shecanic community rallied to console a poster named Mary who tallied up an astronomical list of repairs on her Mini Cooper, but in fact nothing on her list was unusual or uncommon. Still, the $5,000 quote on her six-year-old car was heartbreaking.

Mary's misfortune started when she purchased her car.

A Mini Cooper is a moderately priced vehicle, which many car buyers might think of as a midrange choice. But in fact, a Mini Cooper (while super cute) is also a car that is both unique and European. Its parts, including the engine, are manufactured by BMW. For this reason, the cost of repairs on Mini Coopers can be astronomical.

A car doesn't have to be a luxury model to cost an arm and a leg to maintain and repair. Often European cars come with higher price tags for both parts and labor, and it can be difficult to find qualified technicians to fix them outside the dealerships where they are sold. Being able to afford the car's initial sticker price doesn't mean you'll be able to afford maintenance a few years down the line, and Mary's dilemma is an example of how repair costs can overwhelm you several years after the purchase.

The true cost of owning a car involves many factors besides the initial purchase price. Make sure you understand the prices associated with each when buying a car.

1. Interest on financing—how much the bank that is financing your car loan is charging in interest per year.

2. Depreciation—how much value the car loses each year.

3. Fuel—the gasoline or fuel you need. Does the vehicle require regular or premium?

4. Insurance—auto insurance, including personal liability, collision, comprehensive, and roadside assistance. Don't forget gap insurance, which covers the gap between your insurance plan and your car loan in the event of a total loss. Say, for

example, that you obtain a loan to purchase a new car worth $30,000. After a year, you get into an accident and total the car. Your insurance company values the totaled car at $20,000. But you still owe $25,000 on the car note. Gap insurance covers the $5,000 difference. Without it, you'd have to pay out of pocket.

5. Tags and registration—state vehicle registration renewal, inspections, and emissions tags.

6. Maintenance and repairs—tires, oil changes, and all other maintenance and repairs necessary to keep your vehicle operational. Most luxury brands offer a free short-term maintenance package, normally over the first three years after purchase. But don't assume that three years of "free" maintenance will automatically save you money. Even with their plushy maintenance plans, luxury brands can still be more expensive over the long term, when those repair costs eventually become yours to manage.

Fortunately, a very useful online tool can help you calculate these costs before you contract a case of delayed sticker shock like Mary's. Featuring new and lightly used cars (five years or less), the online True Cost to Own calculator covers the first five years of ownership. Head over to http://www.edmunds.com/tco.html to check it out.

How's My Driving?

In order to determine if you can afford the true cost of a car you want to purchase, you must understand your driving and spending habits. Let's get honest here, #shecanics. What's your current relationship with your car? Do you take good care of it? Drive it responsibly? I abused my cars and still do. I sometimes brake hard,

I strain the transmission by accelerating too fast, I often waste gas by speeding. And in the past I waited until the last minute to take care of maintenance and repairs. I'm a prime candidate for a car that can take a beating, with a long warranty and low repair costs. If you know you are going to beat up the car and are not committed to changing your relationship style, that's your best bet, too.

A car is the most expensive purchase most people make next to a home. And today people are holding on to cars longer than ever before. Are you good at budgeting maintenance and repairs for your car? Are you good at budgeting in general? How long do you plan on keeping the car? How much can you afford to spend on maintenance and repairs over the span of your ownership? All of these concerns factor into the type of car you should buy and whether you can afford its true cost to own. I bought a new car almost every three years because I didn't want to budget repairs into my life. My maintenance and repairs bills were at a minimum, but this isn't a smart money move. I've wasted a lot of money due to my fear of confronting repair costs and mechanics.

Here's where the True Cost to Own calculator comes in handy. Make sure you understand your driving and spending habits and can afford the car before you purchase it. Looking ahead will not only save you from frustrating situations like mine and Mary's down the line, it could also save you from making a poor decision with one of the most expensive purchases of your life.

Pick the Right Point of Purchase

Whether you're starting out with a binder full of consumer reports and a prioritized wish list or a blank slate, one of the most important decisions you'll make is where to shop. These days there are lots of ways to go about buying a new or used car, and each comes with benefits and risks.

At the end of the day, you want a good deal and a great car you can have a long-term, loving relationship with. Where you purchase your car is important, because it can determine whether your relationship with your new car starts off strong.

Car salespeople are experts. It may sound hard to believe, but your salesperson should be your ally, your buddy, your friend. You should establish a good business relationship with him or her and with the entire dealership staff. They are there not only to sell you a car, but also to help you make the right choice for you. Even if you have your car in mind, share your driving and spending habits with them. Listen to their opinions if they differ from yours. An experienced salesperson knows and has seen it all.

If you're someone who has a lot of time to research and shop around for a car to get a great price, there are plenty of online tools to help you find a car and direct you to a dealership. If you're someone like me, who doesn't have a lot of time to spend on this process, a dealership is your best option.

Franchised Dealerships

The only place to shop if you're buying a new car, dealerships have direct relationships with auto manufacturers. Franchised dealers also sell used cars that are mostly under five years old. The benefits of buying from a dealership are clear.

+ Their salespeople not only are experts on the brand you want to buy, like Ford, they are also trained to help you find the right car for your budget and needs.

+ On-site certified technicians look over and fix the car before the sale.

+ They provide financing options.

+ They have direct associations with the auto manufacturers.

+ They have access to discounts and financing deals through the auto manufacturers.

+ They may offer the option to test-drive the car for twenty-four hours or longer.

+ They make trade-ins easy if you're looking to sell your current car, and they also sell certified used cars.

On the minus side:

- Dealerships are often the most expensive places to buy a used car.

- Dealerships are expensive places to maintain and repair your car. Prices at their servicing centers are two or three times those of independent repair shops.

Auto Malls and Large Chains

Megadealerships that carry numerous brands under the same roof, auto malls or large chains can be convenient as one-stop shops for trying out several kinds of used cars. Among their pluses:

+ The salespeople are trained to help you find the right car for your budget and needs.

+ On-site certified technicians look over and fix the car before sale.

+ They provide financing options.

+ Some have no-haggle prices, so you don't have to do any negotiating.

+ They make trade-ins easy if you're looking to sell your current car.

On the minus side:

- Auto malls tend to be just as expensive as franchised dealerships, even though they do carry cars more than five years old.

- Auto malls don't have servicing centers.

Independent Used Car Dealers

Carrying numerous brands under the same roof, independent used dealers can be owned by a single entrepreneur or a group of people acting as a small business. Is their reputation for untrustworthiness deserved? Honestly, I'm not sure if the whole "used car salesman" stigma started with a few bad apples or holds a grain of truth. Like any option, used car dealerships come with their pros and cons. Among the benefits:

+ They offer cars with a wide age range, including cars past three to ten years old. Options can range from less than 10,000 miles to "Next stop, junkyard."

+ They often carry options under $10,000.

+ They tend to be cheaper than dealerships and auto malls.

+ Some indie dealers offer financing options.

On the minus side:

- Their on-site technicians may not be the most qualified techs. You'll have to be more diligent when checking the car over to make sure the quality matches the price.

- They have smaller selections of cars.

- The older the car, the harder to track its maintenance and repair history.

- Financing rates may be significantly higher than those of dealerships or auto malls.

- They may not allow you to test-drive the car overnight or for a longer period.

- You will have to be more diligent with researching the car's history. An indie used car dealer may sell rebuilt, fixed-up cars that have been in accidents. Be sure to check the vehicle's VIN on the website Carfax.com (see page 253) to find out what you're getting into.

Private Owners

You can buy from private owners online, through websites like Craigslist or eBay Motors, from local paper ads, or by word of mouth. The one and only time I bought a car from a private owner, the seller ended up being someone I sorta kinda knew—by association and eventually by reputation—but things didn't turn out so well. You have no idea what you are getting into when you purchase a car from a private owner, so you must be more diligent when researching the car's history and maintenance and repair records. A serious private owner will have most of the research done for you. Here's my take on how it shakes out, starting with the biggest plus:

+ Buying from a private owner offers the single best deal for a used car since there is no middleman. Many people like to sell their cars privately so they can get the best price for themselves, and you'll also be getting the best price for yourself. A private car purchase is the high-risk, high-reward stock of car purchases.

And now for the negatives:

- You must pay cash. (This is more of a positive to me.)

- You must pay a mechanic to look over the car.

- You won't be able to test-drive the car overnight or for a long period of time.

- You will have to be more diligent with researching the car's history. The seller may be selling a car he or she has done lots of work on. Be sure to check the vehicle's VIN on the website Carfax.com (see page 253) to find out what you're getting into.

Buying New

There are many advantages to buying a new car. The new car smell is one of my favorite smells of all time, and it's one of the reasons I purchase new cars. Being free from worry over how a previous owner treated the car is another advantage of buying new. Finally, prices for new cars are pretty standard, and you know you won't have to think about expensive repairs for a few years.

You can buy new cars only from franchised dealerships, and they love to offer all types of deals to get customers to finance or lease a car. You won't need a PCT to look over a new car, and you won't need to invest nearly as much time and energy in researching as you would if buying a used car.

Leasing New

I'm a great candidate for a lease, because I like a new car every two to three years. There are other advantages of leasing a car, including:

- Lower monthly payments with a low (and sometimes no) down payment

- No major repair costs because you are always under the vehicle's included factory warranty

- Easier transition to a new car every two or three years

- Easy and hassle-free trade-in when your lease agreement ends

- Often less sales tax

- Being able to get a nicer, fancier car for less money

Leasing a car sounds great right? But there are some huge downsides:

- You don't own the car. Leasing is like paying rent. You pay to drive the car for three years or less, but in the end you don't own anything. There is always the option to buy the lease after the leasing term is up. But you *never* want to buy your leased car. It will be cheaper to buy the same car used.

- Your car payments will never end.

- Your mileage allowance on a lease is typically 12,000 miles a year. You can purchase extra miles if you need to, but make sure you understand how many miles you will drive per year in the next few years. If you drive 40-plus miles just to go to and from work, with that alone you are cutting close to the 12,000 miles per year mark. Many frequent leasers have secondary, beater cars they use to save miles and wear and tear on the leased car.

- Lease contracts can be confusing and filled with legalese, so make sure you have a great relationship with your salesperson, and don't be afraid to ask questions about your agreement.

- Long term, leasing is more expensive than buying a car and keeping it for years.

- Excessive wear-and-tear charges can be a nasty surprise at the end of the lease.

- It's costly to terminate before your leasing period is up, which you might have to do if your driving needs change.

Leasing is a great option if you like driving a nice luxury car at a low price. However, it isn't the best option for your long-term financial health. Suze Orman definitely advises against it. So if you're not in a jam, and you already own a car, lease a second car. Your older car can be used to fill in when you're not looking for a fancy ride or when you need to make a long trip.

There may be a time when leasing a *used* car is most cost effective for you, but I do not recommend this option unless it is your last resort. Your salesperson can help you determine if this is a good choice depending on your spending and driving habits as well as your budget.

Buying Used: Don't Fear the Used Car Lot

You may have heard the old adage that cars depreciate as soon as we drive them off the lot. Sad but true. Unlike houses or 401(k)s, cars aren't investments that ripen over time. They lose a lot of value their first two years, unless you're talking about a classic or show car. But here's the upside: For the same reason, used cars often represent better value for your money. With a used car, someone else (the car's first owner) already absorbed the cost of driving the car off the lot. Buying used is the way to go if you make the right choice and don't get saddled with expensive repairs. It's the unknowns that are scary.

We don't know whether the previous owner loved and cared for the car the way we plan to. Was that owner a ♪#shecanic, or a certified auto airhead? The answer might not be obvious, but it matters. You have to do more research and be more educated to buy used. That is why I stayed away from used cars. But if you know what you are doing, buying a used car can be great.

While still in school to become a technician, I purchased a used car on Craigslist, looking to bank some hands-on auto tech experience as fast as I could. Before taking the plunge, I had the head of the automotive department look over the car with me. I was aiming to test out my new skills on a hoopty, not wind up with a total clunker.

Turned out my teacher knew the previous owner, a woman who'd brought her car in to the school to get it fixed a bunch of times. He and a teaching assistant looked the car over and gave me some ideas of what it needed—tires, a tune-up, brakes, rotors. Off I went and plunked down some $2,500 for an eleven-year-old Toyota Corolla. When I brought the car back to the lab a few weeks later, my teacher looked at me and said, "I wouldn't have bought that car, definitely not at that price.

"Nope," he continued, shaking his head. "Not the way that woman drives."

He could have been a little bit more helpful by telling me that in the first place. But the good news was, there ended up being plenty for me to work on, including lots of suspension issues. It was my auto airhead karma.

Most of us don't have money to play around with and aren't trying to bank a learning experience. So let's talk about how to make sure you minimize your odds of winding up with a lemon.

Five Ways to Tell Whether You've Found the Used Car of Your Dreams

Once you've found the used car you think you want, it's time to get more serious about this new potential friend. Here's how I assess whether or not I've located my new BFF.

1. Is the price of the car fair, given its condition? Do your research online by using tools like kbb.com, Edmunds.com, or cars.com that help you determine the value of the car you want based on age, miles driven, amenities, and general condition of function and aesthetics (great, good, fair, poor). Some sellers will provide this information for you.

2. Has the car been through a crash or natural disaster? Check Carfax.com to get the car's history (which travels with its VIN), and see whether you can find evidence of significant damage. Often, cars that have suffered major damage have repeating and recurring failures. The car will never be quite right again, so it's generally not worth the risk. Most sellers will provide this information.

3. Show me the receipts! Ask the seller to provide maintenance and repair records from the previous owner or owners. This should be a major selling point for a well-educated ♫#shecanic. Proof that the car was cared for and loved is invaluable. You want to see that all the major maintenance tasks—oil changes, fluid flushes, tune-ups, belt replacements—have been performed regularly. The sparser the records, the more nervous you should be about buying the car.

4. Was the car's exterior well taken care of? No signs of rust on the body or underneath? Do not buy a car with visible rust on its body or undercarriage unless you understand the implications and costs associated with the rust. Cars with extensive rust are more costly to repair. Rust could also compromise the integrity of the car frame.

5. How does the interior look? While an interior that's less than spic-and-span won't affect how the car operates, it might be an indication that the car wasn't well cared for. Plus, your comfort level matters. The cloth ceiling of my '88 Chevy Cavalier loved to lie on my backseat passengers' heads, and I had to thumbtack that thing to the car ceiling. That was fine for a teenager, but today it would be a no-go.

Never, Ever Skip the Test Drive

Once you've picked out a buggy that suits your budget and fits your style, take your prospective ride for a test drive. Make sure you drive for at least thirty minutes. And don't be shy. Open that baby up, take her out on the highway! Drive to a parking lot where you can come to a hard stop, and make a few hard right and left turns. Turn the car off and on a few times. You want to be smelling, feeling, and listening for anything unusual. How does it feel to sit in and drive the car? You want to be comfortable, be able to see clearly on all sides, and feel safe. Here's a checklist of what to listen, look, and feel for when buying a used car.

AC and Heating System

- Is the system functioning? Make sure the heat and AC both work, not only when you're in park, but also while you're driving.

- Do you hear any loud or unusual noises coming from the heater or AC? These may be indications that the blower motor is failing.

- Has the cabin air filter been changed? These should be swapped out about once a year.

Heating and AC repairs can get very expensive. So even though this may seem like a negligible line item, don't buy a car with a non-functional climate control system unless you know what caused the failure and how much it will cost to fix. Negotiate with the seller to deduct the cost of the repair from the price of the car or have the owner fix the issue.

Brakes

- Are the brake pads, rotors, shoes, and fluid new? These should be new or like new, and essentially pristine. (With one exception: Brake shoes don't wear as quickly as brake pads, so cars outfitted with drum brakes may not need that part replaced until after something like 50,000 miles.)

- How does the brake pedal feel? It shouldn't fall to the floor or feel soft or spongy. There should be a nice resistance on your foot when you brake.

- How does the action of the brakes feel during normal braking while driving? You shouldn't feel any pull or shaking.

- How do the brakes respond when you brake hard? The car should come to a quick stop and should never feel unstable or out of control.

- How do the brakes sound? Do they make any grinding or squealing noises? Determine the cause of the noise before you purchase the car.

If the brake pads, rotors, or shoes are not new or like new, have the seller replace them before you buy the car or deduct the price of the service. Don't buy a car that shakes or vibrates when you are braking, or feels like it has any braking issues of any kind. Have the seller get the car fixed and test-drive it again. Brakes are the number one safety feature on a car.

Electrical System

- Do all the exterior and interior lights work? Don't forget the reverse, brake, and turn signal lights in the back.

- When you turn the key in the ignition to the on position without starting the car, does the check-engine light illuminate on the dashboard? If this light does not illuminate, the bulb has been removed or is blown out.

- When you turn on the engine, does the check-engine light stay on? If so, you may have problems.

- Are any other dashboard lights illuminated when they shouldn't be? See the dashboard chapter (page 24) if you need a refresher on what these are.

Have the seller replace any blown-out lights or fix any lighting issues. Do not buy a car from someone who tries to sell it with the check engine lightbulb removed or blown out—this screams *Scam!* Do not buy a car where the check-engine or any other red dashboard light (see dash chapter) is illuminated unless you know what caused the failure and how much it will cost to fix. Deduct the repair from the price of the car or have the seller get the car fixed and confirm the repair.

Steering

- Do you feel unusual looseness or tightness in the steering wheel? These could be signs of a power steering issue.

- Does the car drift or pull to one side while driving? That's usually a sign that the wheels need to be realigned.

- Do you hear any grinding noises while turning? These could be indications that a steering part has failed.

Do *not* buy a car with steering issues! Steering repairs can get very expensive. Have the seller get the car fixed and the wheels aligned (and ask to be shown the receipts), then test-drive it again before taking the plunge.

Suspension

- Do you hear noises while you are driving or turning on bumpy roads? Thumps, creaks, and humming noises on less-than-smooth road conditions are indications that a suspension part has failed.

Do *not* buy a car with suspension issues unless you know what caused the failure and how much it will cost to fix. And don't forget the realignment if it is necessary. Negotiate with the seller to deduct the cost of the repair from the price of the car.

Tires

- Are all four tires new or fairly new? It would be nice for all four tires to match brands, and on an AWD vehicle, it's necessary. If the tires are new but the brands don't match, you ideally want to have two of the same brand on the front wheels and two of the same brand on the back.

- Are the spare tire and tools to change a spare present and in good condition? Have the seller include a spare tire and tools or replace the bad items.

Do *not* buy a car with old tires, or with a crazy mismatched assortment of tires. On the other hand, it's more important to match tire tread thickness than to match brand. Deduct the price of replacing the necessary tires including the spare (if applicable) from the price of the car.

Transmission

- While going from reverse to drive or drive to reverse, does the transmission shift hard?

- Does the rear of an RWD, 4WD, or AWD vehicle make noise when driving or reversing?

- Does the car shift hard while automatically shifting gears?

- Does the car slip while shifting gears?

Do *not* buy a car with any of these transmission problems!

Engine

- Has the car had a recent tune-up? If the car is within 5,000 miles of a scheduled tune-up, you will need to get one soon.

- If the car's mileage is at or over 100,000 miles, has the timing belt been replaced?

- How does the car sound and smell while in drive? Any loud exhaust noises, tapping in the engine, or burned-rubber or sweet-smelling odors are signs of issues with the engine and/or exhaust.

Do *not* buy a car whose timing belt hasn't been replaced unless you are prepared to pay at least $700 for the replacement. Deduct the tune-up and/or repair from the price of the car or have the seller fix it and confirm the repair.

Under the Hood

- Is the battery new? All used cars should come with new batteries. If you purchase a car with a battery that is two years or older, count on replacing it immediately.

- Have the serpentine belt or belts been replaced? All belts should be new, with no cracks.

- Do there appear to be any leaks under the hood? Find out what's causing them and the cost of repair.

- Check the oil dipstick. The oil should be fresh and new, and the dipstick should read full. No exceptions.

- When starting or driving the car, do you hear any high-pitched chirping noises? A serpentine belt or pulley may need to be changed.

- Is the engine air filter new or like new?

- Are the essential fluid reservoirs under the hood full with new or like new fluids? Check the fluids yourself. See the DIY section on page 172 for instructions on how.

Do *not* buy a car whose engine oil is riddled with black specks. That's an indication that the previous owner did not keep up with oil changes and that the engine is now more prone to leaks and performance problems. If any fluids are low, find out why. If any fluids are dirty, they'll need a fluid flush. Deduct the price of the repairs and maintenance from the price of the car or have the seller service the car and confirm the service.

Miscellaneous

- Are the windshield wipers working and new or like new?

- Is the size of the car a good fit for you? Can you adjust the seat so that you'll be comfortable during a long drive?

- How's the visibility? Do you like the height of the car and the seat? Some drivers prefer to sit low, others like to sit high.

That's a long checklist, ♫#shecanics. If you want a little assist, you can plop down thirty to fifty bucks and test-drive the used car right on over to your PCT. He or she will check all of the above and then some, and can give you a price on any repairs needed. Best of all, your PCT can give you an unbiased opinion on whether you should buy the car and if the price is fair.

Smarter Car Purchasing in Eight Easy Steps

The following steps will help you build a lasting, trusting relationship with your ride, with a minimum toll on your wallet.

1. **Find your salesperson/dealership.** I've heard just as many horror stories from women about purchasing a car as I have about repairing one. Often women feel slighted by the salesperson/staff or regret their purchase after problems arise. Making the right choice on where to purchase your car is important. As we've just discussed, there are many places to buy cars these days, including the Internet.

2. **Buy the right car.** Think about what's important to you in a car before you buy it. Besides your preferences in terms of brand, color, and style, you should be thinking about your driving habits, safety, and the true cost to own. If you

are someone who isn't good at budgeting for repairs, you may consider leasing a car or buying a car with a longer warranty and reasonably priced repairs. In other words, a Mercedes might not be the car for you. A Hyundai Elantra is an example of a car with a long warranty and reasonably priced repairs. If you can't afford premium gas or synthetic oil changes, a luxury car is not your best choice. Even used. If you can't afford to get the car fixed, you can't afford the car.

Luxury models like a BMW or a Mercedes carry higher maintenance and repair price tags than mainstream makes like Toyota, Honda, or Ford. But the same holds true of premium and sportier brands like Cadillac or Mustang and for European cars, luxury or standard. Cars made anywhere else in the world (generally Japan, South Korea, or the United States) tend to be engineered following the same principles, while European models follow a different blueprint and require a specialized mechanic. Because they have bigger engines and wheels and more complex transmission systems, SUVs come with a higher true cost to own than sedans. They also use more fluids and fuel, and tend to have additional parts and electrical accessories. Whatever the model, additional amenities such as fog lights, all-wheel drive, and a sunroof not only increase the price of the car but also drive up the cost of repairs. Each of these features represents additional parts, and additional points of failure.

3. Find your PCT. You should locate a PCT as soon as you purchase a car, ideally before. If you are buying a used car, you'll want a PCT to look it over to make sure you are getting a fair price and not buying a lemon. (Getting a mechanic involved when purchasing a new vehicle would be overkill.) If you need help finding a PCT, see page 35. If you already have a PCT, find out what he or she thinks. PCTs have seen it all when it comes to cars, and they can tell you what to expect for repairs and

Where Did My Car Come From?

Interested in a certain brand, but not sure where it's made? Check out this list.

Asian Automakers
Known for practicality

Japan

Honda - Honda Acura (also known for longevity)
Hyundai - Hyundai, Kia
IsuzuMazda (recently owned by Ford, may have Ford parts)
Mitsubishi
Nissan - Nissan, Infiniti, Datsun

South Korea
(longest warranties, practicality)

Suzuki
Toyota- Toyota, Lexus, Scion (also known for longevity)

American Automakers
Known for practicality, trucks, classic, and muscle cars

Fiat Chrysler (Italian-American) - Dodge, Chrysler, Jeep, Ram (American), Fiat, Alfa Romeo, Ferrari (until recently), Maserati (Italian)

Ford - Ford, Lincoln (did make Mercury)

GM - Buick, Chevrolet, Cadillac, GMC (did make Saturn, Pontiac, Hummer)

European Automakers
Known for style and unique engineering. Higher repair & maintenance costs

Germany

BMW - BMW, Mini, Rolls-Royce
Daimler - Mercedes-Benz, Smart Car
VW - Audi, Bentley, Bugatti, Lamborghini, Porsche, Ducati

Britain/India

Jaguar Land Rover

Sweden

Saab
Volvo

maintenance and whether that particular make, model, or year is known for any specific problems. Rule of thumb: If you don't have the time and energy to research a car's cost of ownership, get advice from your PCT. Give him or her a list of the makes and/or qualities you're looking for in a car, and he or she will come up with some great suggestions for reliable cars that don't cost a ton to repair.

4. Know your maintenance schedule. See page 22 for a breakdown of regular maintenance tasks. Keeping on schedule with these will help you avoid costly repairs down the line.

5. Get your oil changed promptly when a change is due. This really falls under the previous point, but this regular checkup is so vital to the health of your car that I had to mention it again.

6. Don't wait until the last minute to get repairs. If you can't afford a repair, ask your PCT what you can do to make sure the car is still safe to drive until you can get the money together. But know that not all repairs can wait.

7. If your car has over 80,000 miles, put additional money aside for repairs or buy an extended warranty. Repairs will arise unexpectedly and can get pricey. Have an emergency fund containing at least 5 percent of the vehicle's value. If the car is worth $10,000, that's around $500. You may also consider buying an extended warranty if you do not budget money well for car repairs. We'll talk more about warranties on the next page.

8. Don't nickel-and-dime. You just spent $30,000 on a car, and now you're trying to find the lowest price to get it maintained and fixed? That's some shady treatment of your investment. Investing in quality maintenance from a trusted PCT is likely to save you money in the long run, so buy a cheaper car if you can't afford the maintenance on yours.

What You Need to Know About Auto Warranties

An auto warranty is a promise, a contract that says the party from whom you've purchased your car will cover repairs and defects over the course of a certain amount of time or mileage. There are two types of car warranties—those offered by auto manufacturers like Ford or Toyota, and the aftermarket warranties provided by third parties not related to the auto manufacturers. Every car comes with a warranty guarantee from the auto manufacturer.

Warranties run out after a certain number of years or miles driven. If something breaks or needs repair beyond the warranty scope, you will have to pay out of pocket. That means if you have a warranty of five years or 60,000 miles and the transmission fails at five years, three months from the date of purchase or at 60,567 miles, you're on your own. The average car owner drives 12,000 miles annually, so auto manufacturers and third-party warranty providers use this as the standard. After this warranty runs out, the driver has the option to purchase an extended warranty to cover the cost of future repairs.

Sounds like a great idea, right? Pay some money now, avoid expensive repairs later? But warranties are tricky if you don't understand them. They aren't always the one-size-fits-all answers they're made out to be. Depending on the fine print, they may or may not cover "wear items," parts like wheel bearings, which are guaranteed to wear over time—and in some cases a dealership could refuse to honor your warranty based on how you cared (or failed to care) for the car.

Neither aftermarket nor auto manufacturer warranties cover regular maintenance items like oil changes and brake pad replacements. Warranties also won't cover breakdowns caused by accidents, acts of nature, lack of proper maintenance, contamination of fluids or fuels, collision, fire, theft, negligence, or abuse.

Let's save you some frustration and misunderstood expectations down the line by learning more about exactly what warranties do mean in terms of repairs on your ride.

Warranties vs. Maintenance Packages

Do not confuse a warranty with a maintenance package from the dealership.

When you purchase a luxury car from a dealership, it will often include a three-year maintenance package. You will not need to pay for oil changes, brake pads, and so on over that period. On standard cars, dealerships tend to offer maintenance packages you can add on at purchase.

Make sure you understand what maintenance is and is not involved. Compare the cost of purchasing the three-year maintenance add-on and that of taking the car to your PCT over the next three years. It may not be cheaper to purchase the dealership's maintenance package, especially if you finance the car and add the package to the purchase price. You will be paying interest on the add-on package.

Auto Manufacturer Warranties

Drivetrain/Powertrain Warranty. Your vehicle's powertrain is very important to warrant, because it involves the most expensive parts of your car—the engine, main transmission, and anything that gives power to the wheels, like differentials. Most cars come with a manufacturer's powertrain warranty of five years or 60,000 miles, whichever comes first. If any powertrain parts fail before then, the manufacturer will cover the cost of the repair.

Basic "Bumper-to-Bumper" Warranty. Also called a comprehensive warranty, the bumper-to-bumper warranty covers the cost of repairs for almost every part on your car from the front bumper to the rear bumper, minus the powertrain. (The powertrain is covered by a separate warranty.) If any factory-installed parts fail, from the audio system to suspension parts, the cost of repair or replacement should be covered by the manufacturer. All cars come with at least a three-year or 36,000-mile bumper-to-bumper warranty, whichever comes first. This type of warranty does *not* include tires, which often get a warranty of 12,000 miles or less. Check your handy-dandy owner's manual to find out what is covered in your bumper-to-bumper warranty. The bumper-to-bumper warranty doesn't last as long as the powertrain warranty because it covers many more parts on the car.

Add-Ons. There are some warranty add-ons you may be able to purchase, such as rust/corrosion warranties or federal emissions warranties. Primary care technicians don't tend to recommend these, and I think you should trust us.

TIP: *What if you buy a gently used, two-year-old car? Auto manufacturers' warranties stay with the VIN of the car (not its owner or driver), so they transfer with the sale of a car. If a used car hasn't reached the auto manufacturer's warranty limit, the warranty is still valid.*

Extended and Aftermarket Warranties

Aftermarket warranties, sometimes called extended warranties, are warranty packages that dealerships and independent dealers sell through third-party companies. An extended warranty serves as a patch job for the period after the manufacturer's initial warranty runs out. Extended warranties can be bought at any time—at initial purchase or later down the line.

An extended auto warranty may seem like exactly what you need, especially as the costs of repairing a vehicle keep rising. There are many advantages and disadvantages to aftermarket warranties, and buying one for your car depends on your driving and spending habits.

Advantages of an Aftermarket Warranty

- Relieves the stress that comes with car repair

- Can be purchased at any time

- Good for luxury and European cars with more expensive repairs. (Mary could have used an aftermarket warranty.)

- Better options for people who aren't committed to taking care of their cars or aren't budgeting for repairs

Disadvantages of an Aftermarket Warranty

- Warranty companies pay the mechanic or shop who performs the repair, not the person who purchased the warranty. You may have to pay for the repair up front and get reimbursed or wait until the company approves the claim and pays the mechanic; not all mechanics will work with aftermarket warranties. The arrangement involves a lot of paperwork, and sometimes the company will send out an inspector to confirm the damage and repair costs.

- Aftermarket warranty companies are often like dodgy insurance companies—they'll look for every excuse under the sun to avoid paying for the repair you try to claim.

- You will have to pay a deductible.

- You may have to pay some of the repair costs after the deductible.

- The warranty company may select where the warranty repair must be performed, so you might not be able to take your car to your PCT.

- Unlike auto manufacturer warranties, aftermarket warranties may not be transferable with the sale of a car.

Three Times When an Aftermarket Warranty Is a Good Idea

- Consider purchasing an aftermarket warranty on luxury or European cars that you plan on keeping past 100,000 miles. No matter how well you take care of your car, repairs on luxury and European cars can be expensive.

- If you don't have a PCT, get a warranty. If you shop-hop, you never know who is working on your car. Often mechanics make mistakes that you won't see until later, increasing your risk of expensive repairs as the car ages.

- If you are not committed to taking care of your car or putting money aside for repairs after 80,000 miles, get an aftermarket warranty.

When Warranties Get Tricky

Here's a question I am asked frequently: *Am I voiding my warranty by taking my car to an outside repair shop for maintenance and service instead of to the dealership or preferred shop?* The answer is no. Repairs that are *not* covered by the warranty, aka nonwarranty repairs, can be done anywhere. All maintenance can be done elsewhere as well.

An auto manufacturer warranty is with the manufacturer (Ford), not the dealership, so it will remain valid no matter who performs the nonwarranty repairs, meaning you can use your preferred PCT and don't have to stick with the dealer's service department.

If you need a warranty repair covered by the auto manufacturer performed on the car, take it to the dealership. There's a lot more paperwork required in trying to get reimbursed for a warranty repair done at an independent shop, and auto manufacturers will accept repairs only from preapproved shops.

Both auto manufacturer and aftermarket warranties may require you to use a certain oil for oil changes and/or perform maintenance at scheduled periods. Pay attention to the warranty's conditions and make sure you *keep your receipts*! Just like the insurance industry, the auto warranty industry will use fine print and your driving habits to get out of paying for a job or paying the full amount for a job. Aftermarket warranty companies may send inspectors out to confirm the damage and prove the driver had no fault.

If you can't show you held up your end of the warranty, like having regular scheduled maintenance performed per your owner's manual, they may not pay for the repair.

How to Know It's Time to Say Good-bye

How do you end a love affair with the best friend you've hung out with almost every day for the past several years of your life? Break-ups are really hard. And letting go can be downright terrifying.

Letting go of a car? Never a problem for me! Just the opposite, in fact. I was often a bit too hasty in my quest to move on, buying a new car as soon as my old friend showed any signs of wear. How unloyal I was back then. In my fortune-teller's ball I saw multiple trips to the mechanic, stacks of bills for multi-hundred-dollar repairs, and breakdowns at the worst possible times. So I ran in the other direction.

As your car accumulates more and more miles, many of its parts begin to wear down and fail. Every moving part on your car will fail eventually. That's a certainty. And there comes a point when, every time you turn around, your car needs to go back in the shop for a $750 repair or you get slammed with one big $2,000-plus bill.

How are you supposed to know when to call it quits and trade in your car? The 100,000-mile mark is a good rule of thumb. After this point, nothing will be covered by the warranty, and repair costs will begin to mount. On the flip side, most drivers have paid off their car loans by this point, and the cost of insurance will be lower. Some people are lucky enough to be able to purchase a new car whenever they please. But often, buying a new (or new-to-you) vehicle represents a serious monetary load, so the decision will have to involve some number crunching.

Need-to-Know Facts

Before you purchase a car, new or used, make sure you understand the following about the warranty:

1. The length of the warranty
2. The point of contact for service or repair
3. What parts and repair problems are covered
4. Any conditions or limitations on the warranty

Ask your salesperson to explain in detail what the warranty covers, and read the warranty. Boring, but important. Like health benefits and retirement plans in a job offer scenario, the fine print here may actually help determine the difference between a good deal and a money drainer.

Choosing a Car for Its Warranty

Selecting a new car based on the strength of its warranty is a great strategy for a budget-minded ♪♯shecanic. Some of the best auto manufacturer warranties on the market today (Kia, Hyundai, and Mitsubishi come to mind) run for ten years or 100,000 miles on the powertrain, and five years or 60,000 miles for bumper to bumper.

The standard warranty for auto manufacturers would get you three years or 36,000 miles bumper to bumper, and five years or 60,000 miles on the powertrain (think Honda, Nissan, Toyota, Ford, Mazda, and Subaru).

Let Your PCT Come to the Rescue

Still can't tell whether it's time to say good-bye? Put it on your PCT. It feels great not to have to figure this one out all on your own, and this is another instance in which developing a long-term relationship with a trusted PCT will pay off. An experienced person who knows your car history and your driving and spending habits should be able to make the call relatively quickly on when it's time for you to move on. He or she may even be able to help you find a used car.

So buy your PCT a cake for her birthday. Send him a check for twenty dollars for Christmas. PCTs are your new everyday heroes.

Your car salesperson can help, too. If you have a relationship with a car salesperson or dealership you trust, it's a great idea to ask for their advice on if you can afford a new or new-to-you car. A great salesperson will work hard to find you a good deal on a car that works for you.

. . . Or Get Out Your Calculator

It might seem like a terribly complicated decision, but there are really only two factors to consider in determining whether it's time to send your baby to the junkyard or if you should try to keep the love alive.

1. What is the cost of owning your current vehicle? How much do you currently pay per year in maintenance, repairs, gas, registrations, dealing with breakdowns, insurance, not to mention the headache of constant repairs? Reflect back on the last two years. As cars age, $500 and $600 repairs become common, and they add up real quick. Major repairs like engine leaks or power steering rack replacements can cost over $1,500. The numbers are likely to be increasing and will continue to increase as the car ages or if it wasn't well taken care of. Your PCT can help you determine what this number is. Your owner's manual will help you determine what maintenance procedures are coming up.

2. What is the true cost to own a new or new-to-you car? Head back to the true-cost-to-own section on page 241 to figure that out. If the current cost to own your car per year is comparable to that of a new or new-to-you car, that's a deal breaker.

What if you have one or several repairs that are adding up to thousands of dollars, like in Mary's example, that you can't afford to pay? Should you break up with your car then? Say you've got a repair bill costing $1,500, plus another $800 to $1,000 for expected repairs and maintenance over the next year on a car that's worth $5,000. It's probably time to say to your car, "It's not me, it's you." How did I come to that conclusion?

By crunching the numbers using this simple equation as a general guideline:

If the price of current repair + current cost to own the car per year > half the value of the car, then the repairs are probably not worth the price.

To put that in plain English: If the cost of maintenance and repairs is greater than half the value of the car, you're probably better off walking away.

In our hypothetical case, $1,500 + $1,000 adds up to $2,500—which is equal to half the value of a $5,000 car.

Some of us are trigger-happy when it comes to getting rid of cars, while others have a hard time letting go. But being a good friend to your wallet means always considering the longer-term costs of your decisions as a car owner.

Sell

You've decided you're ready to get a new car. But what do you do with your old one? You have two options. You can sell it personally or trade it in at a dealership.

Most people trade in their cars at dealerships because it's pretty much hassle-free. The dealer will deduct the cost of the trade-in on your final car purchase. If you want to sell your car personally, you'll likely need to post an ad online.

There are numerous online tools that help you determine the current price of your car, find a dealer that will buy your trade-in, and/or post your car for sale. Websites like Kelley Blue Book, Edmunds, and Autotrader are very helpful. While you're there, you can gather information on finding your new baby.

Good luck, ♪#shecanics!

What to Do in an Emergency

Emergencies like car accidents or breakdowns can't be predicted. If they could, we'd figure out how to avoid them. But a well-rounded 𝄞#shecanic is always a step ahead of any possible incidents on the road thanks to her knowledge and preparations. Read through this chapter to make sure that you already know what to do in a moment of crisis.

General Rules for Any Car Emergency

- Do not panic. It is important that you stay calm so you can make rational decisions.

- Put your hazard lights on immediately to alert other drivers that you are in an emergency situation.

- Pull off to the side of the road as soon as it is safely possible to do so, and apply your parking/emergency brake. Ideally, you want to pull off on level ground with enough space on each side of the car to work safely. If you have a flat tire, pull off the road on the same side as the tire repair. You don't want to change a tire with your back to the passing traffic.

- If you don't feel comfortable getting out of the car to check out what is going on, stay in or close to the vehicle (as long as it is safe and you don't see or smell any signs of smoke or fire) and call for help.

- Otherwise, get out of the car and put out any reflective triangles, flares, or orange cones you have to alert traffic.

- Dial 911 and ask for help if you feel unsafe.

- Find any emergency numbers you may need—towing company, roadside assistance, insurance company, et cetera.

If You Get in a Car Crash

With apologies to your car, the best-case scenario for any crash is that it be minor enough that you are still mobile and lucid. You don't have to call the police after a minor accident, if you and the other party can move your cars safely out of the way of traffic. (Police may still come to help out if they observe the accident.) The police *should* be called if the accident is impeding traffic or is a safety concern.

Here are the things you should do if you are in an accident.

1. Move your vehicle safely out of the way of traffic, if possible, and turn off the car. Catch your breath.

2. Apply the emergency or parking brake and turn on your hazard lights.

3. Make sure no one in the car is hurt. If you or anyone is hurt, call 911.

4. Get out of the car and put out any flares or orange cones you have to alert traffic of an emergency situation. Check the vehicle over for the damage.

5. If you crashed into another vehicle or vehicles, exchange information with the other driver or drivers. Ask for the drivers' license and insurance information and record their names, addresses, phone numbers, insurance companies and policy numbers, the VINs of their cars, and their license plate numbers and states.

6. If the name on the driver's license doesn't match the name on the insurance policy, get the name and contact information of the policyholder.

7. Use your cell phone to take pictures of any damage to both cars. It might also be helpful to take pictures of the surrounding area to help explain how the accident happened, especially if there is a disagreement on who's at fault.

8. Let's be honest, ∫#shecanics, getting in a car crash can be scary if the other vehicle's driver is aggressive or gives you a bad vibe. If you don't feel comfortable, stay in your car with the doors locked and call the police.

9. Call for a tow truck if your car is not drivable.

If Your Engine Overheats

As soon as you see the needle on your temperature gauge creep up past the middle, your engine is in danger of being permanently damaged. You may notice smoke coming out from under the hood. On some cars, the check-engine light will come on. Here are the steps you should take in this situation.

1. Pull over as soon as it is safely possible.

2. Turn the engine off, but put the heat on full blast. This will help move heat away from the engine.

3. Let your vehicle cool down for at least twenty minutes.

4. Open the hood and see what is going on. Check the coolant reservoir. Is there coolant in it? Do not drive a car without coolant. Add some if you have some in the car. Water can be used in an emergency *only*.

5. Look for any coolant under the hood to help determine if there is a leak and how bad it is. If you see neon-colored liquid in puddles in and around other parts under the hood, you likely have a coolant leak somewhere in the system.

6. If you don't have coolant or water, call a tow truck to have your car delivered to your PCT or the nearest shop.

7. If you have coolant or water to add to the coolant reservoir until it is full, start the engine. Let the engine sit until the temperature gauge is right in the middle.

If the temperature gauge starts to creep up past the middle again, turn the car off and call for a tow truck. If the needle on the temperature gauge stays steady in the middle for five minutes, drive your car to your PCT as soon as possible. If the engine starts to overheat again as you are driving, follow steps 1 through 3 and call a tow truck.

If You Lose Brakes While Driving

While this is an uncommon emergency, brakes *can* go out while you're driving, and it's a possibility for which you should be prepared. It is important to try to remain as calm as as you can and remember that you must pump the brake pedal, not slam it.

1. Put the car in neutral as soon as you notice that the brakes are not working.

2. Pump your brakes to slow down. Do not slam them.

3. Once you are at 15 miles an hour or below, slowly apply the emergency brake until the car can stop.

4. Call a tow truck and get your car towed to your PCT ASAP.

If You Have a Flat Tire

See page 203.

If Your Vehicle Won't Start

This will be your mostly likely car emergency, but you won't need to call for help if you have the right knowledge and tools. Even if you get the car started, though, you must determine what caused it not to start; otherwise it could happen again when you least expect it.

There are three things that cause a car not to start.

1. There is no power to turn the starter motor on because of a battery or alternator failure or an electrical or computer issue.

2. The starter motor has failed.

3. The engine is not getting air or fuel to eat.

What do you hear when you turn the key in the ignition?

- If you hear a *tick-tick-tick* or a splutter, the battery needs a jump.

- If you hear nothing but see all the dashboard lights turn on, the battery needs a jump.

- If you hear nothing and see *none* of the dashboard lights come on, the battery may be completely dead, or the starter motor has failed. Try to jump-start the battery. If a jump doesn't work, the battery, alternator, or starter may need a replacement, or you may have an electrical or computer issue. Call for a tow truck to deliver your car to your PCT.

- If you hear a really slow crank or slow start when you turn the ignition, the battery needs a jump-start. Have your PCT check your charging system.

- If you hear a real crank (*chug-chug-chug*), like your car is trying to turn on but the engine just doesn't start, the engine is either not getting air or fuel to eat, or you have an electrical or computer issue. There could be a number of reasons for this. First, make sure it's not because you ran out of gas. If the problem is not that simple, call for a tow truck.

Your PCT can run a quick charging system test to determine whether your car's failure to start is the fault of the battery or alternator. A failed starter is a pretty quick diagnosis as well. If the problem is an air or fuel delivery issue or an electrical or computer issue, this will take some time to diagnose.

If You Need a Tow

It is nice to have a local towing company you can call if your car breaks down or is not drivable. If you need a towing company, your PCT can recommend one. Keep their information in your glove box.

The towing company should ask whether your car is two-wheel drive, four-wheel drive, or all-wheel drive. Four-wheel-drive and AWD vehicles require a flatbed truck to tow them. Two-wheel-drive vehicles can be towed with a wheel-lift tow truck or a flatbed truck. Towing a car incorrectly could damage your transmission.

4WD and AWD vehicles should be
towed on a flatbed truck.

FWD vehicles must be towed backward, and
RWD vehicles must be towed forward.

The Well-Stocked Vehicle

There are some nonnegotiable essentials every #shecanic should keep in her car's glove box and trunk at all times. And there are some other nice-to-have items for overachievers. Putting some of these together into a gift basket is a wonderful gesture for brand-new drivers and grizzled road warriors alike.

Glove Box: Nonnegotiable Essentials

Napkins/rag
Small flashlight
Small first-aid kit
Important phone numbers
Tire pressure gauge
Owner's manual
Proper paperwork: insurance
and registration card
Car charger
Cell phone
Pens
Small pad to write on

Trunk: Nonnegotiable Essentials

Full first-aid kit (a small one should be kept in the glove box in case you can't get to the trunk)

All the equipment and tools to change a flat tire:
Spare tire
Lug wrench
Jack

Trunk: Nice-to-Have Items
Jumper cables
Warning sign: small traffic cones, a flare, or a reflector triangle
Extra oil and coolant if the car has over 100,000 miles
Water
Extra clothes, shoes, and blankets in the winter
Duct tape
Large flashlight

*Never underestimate the power
of duct tape.*

DIY #8: How to Jump-Start a Car

Don't you wish that if your cell phone lost power, you could just touch it to your friend's and have her phone bump some juice over to yours? That's essentially what a jump-start is: a buddy coming to the rescue, giving you juice from his or her alternator to charge your battery so your car has enough electrical power to start.

Tools

Two people
An extra functioning car of any type
Jumper cables

1. Position the front of the car with the properly functioning battery as close as possible to the front of your stalled car, whether head-to-head or side-to-side. Jumper cables are several feet long, though, so they can reach some distance.

2. Pop open both hoods and locate the battery on both cars.

3. Turn both cars off all the way—making sure all electronic accessories such as radios, automatic lights, and AC are turned off on both cars. Engage the parking brakes on both cars.

4. Place one end of the red (aka "dead") clip on the red or positive or plus terminal of the stalled battery (see image, opposite, for additional guidance).

5. Place the other end of the red clip on the red or positive or plus terminal of the working battery.

6. Place one end of the black clip on the black or negative or minus terminal of the working battery.

7. Connect the other end of the black clip to the black or negative or minus terminal of the stalled battery. (To avoid causing a small spark, you can also connect the clip to an unpainted metal bolt on your engine block, but that's an advanced move.)

8. Turn the car with the working battery on and let the engine run for at least a minute. Give this car some gas to lightly rev up the engine.

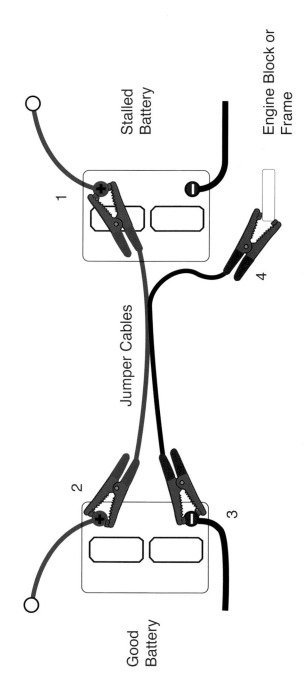

Stalled Battery

Engine Block or Frame

1

Jumper Cables

4

2

3

Good Battery

Assuming the problem car is to the right, here's an overview of the correct cable position to jump-start a car.

9. Turn on the car with the stalled battery.

10. If the car starts, remove the jumper cable clips in the *opposite* order in which you attached them: the black clip on the stalled battery, the black clip on the working battery, the red clip on the working battery, and lastly the red clip on the stalled battery.

Let your car run for at least twenty minutes so the alternator can charge up the battery. Go for a spin, getting out onto a highway if you can. If you turn the car off before the battery can sufficiently charge, you may need to jump-start the car again.

If the car does *not* start, make sure the jumper cable clips are correctly connected to the battery terminals. The metal clips should be touching the metal terminals. Let the cars stay connected, allowing the car with the working battery to run for a few more minutes until your battery gets enough juice to start your car. Depending on how weak your battery or the cables are, this process can take thirty seconds to ten minutes.

If your car won't start after a second try, you likely need a new battery.

Graduation Time

Congratulations, ♪#shecanics. You embarked on an empowering journey of auto care knowledge, and you stuck with it to the finish line. But this journey, which started with a renewed commitment to maintaining your ride, doesn't end with the last pages of this book. It's a ride-or-die kind of thing. So keep in touch with the @girlsautoclinic and ♪#shecanic community on Facebook, Twitter, Instagram, and beyond. Share your triumphs, frustrations, and questions. 'Cause one thing is for sure—we'll always have one another's backs.

And now, in honor of your hard work, it is my pleasure to welcome you to the ranks of the certified ♪#shecanics.

Certificate of Completion and General Awesomeness

_____ is hereby certified as a lifelong

♪#shecanic. She has demonstrated her ability to tell car care

myths from auto maintenance facts, and she pledges never to be

intimidated by her ride.

Note: This certificate never expires, even if its owner

occasionally procrastinates on nonurgent maintenance tasks.

Happy driving!

Acknowledgments

Safiya Simmons of SJS Consulting, thank you for being the first person to believe in *Girls Auto Clinic Glove Box Guide*. You gave me the most significant gift anyone can give an entrepreneur: a lesson about the responsibility of paying it forward. I take that responsibility very seriously.

Savannah Ashour, I am so proud of this book. Thank you.

Dianne Castillo, thank you for stepping up to the plate, making it work, and creating the illustrations on such a tight schedule.

Thank you to Susan Sweeney and Sean Johnson for having my back, and to my agent, Eric Myers, for discovering me.

I appreciate the hard work and encouragement of everyone at Touchstone—especially Matthew Benjamin and Lara Blackman, who got us through to the finish line, and Lorie Pagnozzi for her design. I can't believe I wrote a book in the middle of launching a start-up. I lived like a college student again—broke, hungry, tired, recycling outfits, less frequent showers, frozen pizza for dinner and breakfast. There is nothing sexy about the grind, but in these moments I felt like a writer. I'm humbled and grateful for this experience.

DIY Index

About the Author

Patrice Banks is the founder of Girls Auto Clinic, a female empowerment company that educates and empowers women through their cars. After working for twelve years as an engineer, Banks went back to school for auto repair and began leading car-care workshops, blogging car tips, and inspiring women to get their hands dirty. Now she runs an auto repair shop/salon outside of Philadelphia staffed by female mechanics. She hopes to reach every woman driver with her message.